This book is dedicated to

Cynthia Anne Harrell

October 30, 1985 – January 1, 1997

the one whose life and death

has been an encouragement

to everyone she met in person

and through her powerful story.

CYNDY'S BLESSED ASSURANCE

by Anne H. Harrell & Larry E. White, M.D.

A LEGACY BOOK

Published by Köehler Books
210 60th Street
Virginia Beach, Virginia 23451
www.koehlerbooks.com

Printed and distributed by
Lightning Source and Ingram Books

ISBN 978-0-9765932-7-0

Will I Ever be Whole Again, Copyright 1999, by Sandra P. Aldrich
Published by Howard Publishing Company, Inc.

Let's Study 1Peter, Copyright 2004 by William W. Harrell
The Banner of Truth Trust, 3 Murrayfield Road, Edinburgh EH126EL, UK
PO Box 621 Carlisle, PA 17013, USA

Blessed Assurance, Copyright Fannie Crosby

Sit Down, God, I'm Angry, Copyright 1997 by RF Smith
Published by Judson Press

The Holy Bible, English Standard Version® (ESV®)
Copyright © 2001 by Crossway,
a publishing ministry of Good News Publishers.

Edited by Katie Adams
Cover and text design by John Koehler
Back cover photo by Rob Tankard

For more information about this book and all other inquiries,
contact John Koehler: john@koehlerbooks.com   757-289-6006
www.koehlerbooks.com

AUTHORS' ACKNOWLEDGEMENTS

Many people helped us with this book – they prayed and made suggestions and worked long hours with us to see that Cyndy's life story lives on. It has been a long time coming. We are finally there! We give thanks to the One that inspired us - Jesus Christ - for all His grace and love He has bestowed on us. We give God all the Glory!

Larry and I would first like to thank our spouses Jackie White and Mark Harrell Sr. and our families and extended family for all their support and prayers. They have stood beside us and encouraged us to keep going, listened to rewrites and given their thoughts when asked. Love You Mark! Love You Jackie! (A BIG thank you goes to Jackie for putting back in order the chart when I had dropped it before giving it to the wonderful Doc!). Thanks also to Monica Eaker for the support, prayers, and encouragement after Cyndy's death and while this book was being written.

Others we like to thank are Pastor Mark Bender and the congregation of Calvary Presbyterian Church and Gina Tuck for all the help she gave us getting Cyndy's Blessed Assurance in the works.

We appreciate Dr. Bobby Garrison, Dr. Tony Thomas, Dr. Victor Mickunas, Dr. Kitty Meredith, Dr. Carolyn Riegle, and the staff at Pediatrics Associates for all their support, understanding and care through the years. Kudos to Children's Hospital of Kings Daughters (CHKD) of Norfolk, Virginia for the super care they gave Cyndy.

We are greatly indebted to Family Centered Services: Joan, Janet, Dale, Debbie, Kathleen, Ken and Vick; and Marty Houston at the department of Social Services for their support getting us back on our feet. And also our "family" at Family Solutions, Jack, Stacy and Heather, Bryan, Kent, and Ray. A special thank you to Dr. Coleman; you are the greatest. Many thanks, Rob Tankard for your great photos.

Our biggest thanks go to John Koehler and Katie Adams, Publisher and Editor for Koehler Books. Thank you Katie and John for all you have done to help us get Cyndy's Blessed Assurance published. We could not have gotten the book published and printed without your work, help, and encouragement.

"that their hearts may be encouraged, being knit together in love, to reach all the riches of full assurance of understanding and the knowledge of God's mystery, which is Christ, in whom are hidden all the treasures of wisdom and knowledge."
Col. 2:2-3

The moment your child dies, there is nothing that family members, friends or strangers can say that will take the pain away. My husband and I weren't able to comprehend that our daughter Cyndy was really gone and in heaven that New Year's Day 1997. We couldn't find peace; we wanted our child to be with us here on earth, not somewhere where we could not see or touch her.

My name is Anne Harrell and this is my story. It has taken me a lot of years before I was ready to talk or write about Cyndy's death. When the Lord placed a heavy burden on my heart to write a book on the life and death of His special servant I argued with Him. I did not know when to shut my mouth; I dug myself deeper and deeper pleading with Him "I am not an author...I do not know anything about writing a book! I am not worthy of writing a book for Your glory Lord."

The truth is it hurt me too much to write about Cyndy. My heart bleeds every time I think about her...how could I put into words the blessed assurance and grace and love she had for people? For several restless nights I got on my knees and pleaded with the Lord, "You are the author of the beginning and the end; the Alpha and Omega...You Lord would have to help me, guide me, and hold me when the pain becomes unbearable...if it is Your will for the book to be written, I will abide." Having no idea where to turn or which direction the book should go, I decided just to do as the Lord had called me to do.

When I finally gave in and agreed to write the book the Lord swung doors wide open. I contacted Cyndy's pediatrician Dr. Bobby Garrison and he liked the idea of honoring Cyndy with a book on her life. He was willing to help by giving me Cyndy's medical charts and he encouraged me to ask Dr. Larry E. White, Cyndy's pediatric neurologist, to help as well. Dr. White knew Cyndy well and loved her dearly.

When I called Dr. White it had been three years since Cyndy's death. He didn't know that the Lord had laid it on my heart to ask him to coauthor the book with me. I told him about wanting to write a book on Cyndy's life and that I had some medical questions about her death. He answered my questions and then when I got to the big question about wanting him to co-author the book with me he blurted out yes he would love to coauthor the book. Dr. White told me whatever it took to help me deal with Cyndy's death he would help me through the grief and pain. God had already prepared him to accept my offer. He did not even think about it for a second before yes slipped out of his mouth.

Our family at Calvary Presbyterian Church has also been a great encouragement. Pastor Bender and Gina Tuck from Calvary became involved in this book and many friends shared touching stories of how Cyndy touched their hearts, like our close friend John Leggore who said:

"I've heard some people say that children are the flowers of a couple's love. You can tell a lot about a couple by the way their children act and react to the world. When I first saw Cyndy Harrell at our church in Virginia, I knew that her parents must be loving and kind people. Cyndy seemed so content and happy, and she was warm and friendly to strangers. I did not know the Harrell family then; when I finally got to know them, I found out that my first assessment was correct. Mark and Anne love all their children equally, regardless of how God made them.

As I watched Cyndy play in the church nursery, I could see how different she was from the other children, yet how much she was also like them. Cyndy showed me that I did not have to be nervous or uncomfortable about approaching people who are not 'normal' by the world's standards. One time at church, there was a shortage of people who were available to hold and rock the children to sleep. Something compelled me to offer my lap and shoulder to Cyndy so that she could sleep. I believe God was working on me that day, through Cyndy, to help me become a better person. She sat on my lap without a word and accepted me for who I was, though she did not know me. Talk about a humbling experience. When the service was over, I gave her to her parents and felt much better about life.

Since then, whenever opportunities arise, I try to do at least a little something for others. I even volunteered with Special Olympics. I do not think I would have without my experience with Cyndy. If children like Cyndy have a purpose here, I think it is to humble the rest of us and remind us what is important. I hope God continues to use Cyndy's memory to remind people like me how to truly love others."

It has taken 10 years to write this book. Countless times it seemed like we would not be able to complete and publish it. Yet all along I had an unwavering faith and felt that God would remove any hurdle to make our path smooth. That has been proven true. God has held this book together. We give God the glory for this book and pray that you will be blessed as you read about one of God's servants, a severely handicapped child, who did His will by touching lives throughout her life and even now many years after her death.

The working title of this book was "All for the Love of Cyndy" because everyone could see Cyndy's love for people. But after years of working on the book we realized that it was not Cyndy's love that made this story so special, but rather it was the *Lord's* love for this special child. Cyndy showed us *God's* special love and what childlike faith is all about.

We changed the title of the book when Dr. White heard my youngest daughter Katie play the old hymn "Blessed Assurance" on her viola for offertory at church one Sunday morning. He leaned over told me to listen to the lyrics of the song. As I turned and looked at him, he was crying. I listened closely and realized how beautiful the song is. Cyndy has that assurance now that she is with her Lord. She is at rest with her Savior in perfect peace and happiness. What could be a more appropriate title than "Cyndy's Blessed Assurance?"

So go get your box of tissues, have a seat, and enjoy getting to know Cyndy as we knew her. You may cry a little and I hope you laugh a lot. You will see unbelievable things that happened over Cyndy's short life. I hope the next time you hear "Blessed Assurance," you will stop and listen to the lyrics and let Cyndy come to your mind. Be grateful for the assurance *she* has now, the assurance *we* can have in Christ.

> *"Truly, I say to you, unless you turn and become like children, you will never enter the kingdom of heaven. Whoever humbles himself like this child is the greatest in the kingdom of heaven." - Matthew 18:3-4*

Prayer:
Thank You Father for the love you have shown us through the loss of your special child. Give us the strength to take one-step at a time and know that You are there with us. You are the ONE that holds our hand when the tears fall. We know that joy will come in the morning.

In Christ only,
AMEN

*Cyndy was a special gift to her family
and the many people who came to know and love her.*

*Cyndy was not only willing to receive love
but so generously gave her love to others in return.
Even while trying hard to retain her strength and
having spent many days in her own little world,
she still touched many lives with love and joy as
she passed out her hugs and kisses
to her loved ones.*

*We can remember Cyndy as we look
out in the night sky and see that new star.
That star that reminds us of our Cyndy
as she now shines in heaven*

Written by Cyndy's aunt,
Mary H. Parrish
January 2, 1997

The many faces of

Cynthia Anne Harrell

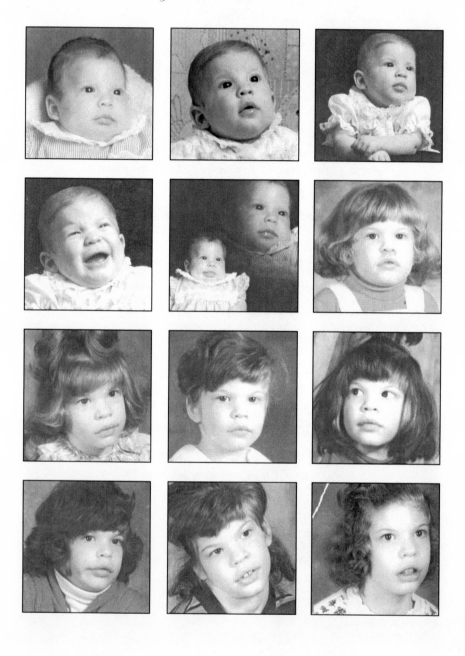

TABLE OF CONTENTS

Blessed Assurance

by Frances J. Crosby

Blessed assurance, Jesus is mine!
O what a foretaste of glory divine!
Heir of salvation, purchase of God,
born of his Spirit, washed in his blood.

Perfect submission, perfect delight,
visions of rapture now burst on my sight;
angels descending bring from above
echoes of mercy, whispers of love.

Perfect submission, all is at rest;
I in my Savior am happy and blest,
watching and waiting, looking above,
filled with his goodness, lost in his love.

Refrain:
This is my story, this is my song,
praising my Savior all the day long;
this is my story, this is my song,
praising my Savior all the day long.

Cyndy's
blessed assurance

A Child Who Challenged Limits and Changed Lives

Anne H. Harrell and Larry E. White, M.D.

KOEHLER BOOKS OF VIRGINIA BEACH   2011

We all have, in our individual or collective memory, dates that bring to mind great joy or sadness: birthday versus tax filing day for example or December 25 versus September 11. Until 1997 January 1st was for me, a day of parades, overeating, and football; but that particular day, part of me died.

My name is Larry White, and I am a doctor specializing in child neurology, treating youngsters with a variety of problems caused by faulty or injured brains, spinal cords, nerves, and muscles. I have been a doctor for over 30 years and a neurologist for over 20, and I love every one of my kids (as I call my patients). They have given me love, joy, patience, confusion, aggravation, frustration, despair, and hope; I have tried to return the love, joy, patience, and hope. Rarely, one of your kids gives you something you never expected: they connect with you in such a way that a physician should never let happen, because you know things you shouldn't know, and likely cannot change. For me, that was Cyndy—with a Y.

I was introduced to Cyndy when she was two years old, after she had one in a series of prolonged, life-threatening convulsions. She wasn't responding well to medications to suppress her seizures, especially when she had a fever or was sick, so I met with the family to outline a strategy. That meeting started a long relationship between Cyndy, her parents and me. Our relationship grew to involve Cyndy's many crises, her brothers' issues with autism and mental challenges, her mom and dad's health issues, and coordination of age-related therapies with her pediatricians, therapists, and social services. Over those years a lot of things happened both good and bad, and as she and the family grew, I grew as a physician and advocate. By her 10th birthday, we thought we had things under control. Then she died...suddenly...unexpectedly...except to me. I had sensed something bad was coming but could not prevent it.

Cyndy's mom, Anne, struggling with her own problems with obsessive compulsive disorder (OCD), bipolar disorder and post traumatic stress disorder, reacted predictably and heroically at times. However it wasn't possible for her to manage her own health issues, her grief over Cyndy, as well as her other children and her own husband who became disabled with heart disease. She couldn't handle everything at first, but slowly things changed. With help from the church, the Bible, friends, doctors, and psychologist/therapists the family reunited, her other kids grew and time passed. But Anne needed closure and an answer to the question we struggled with the day of Cyndy's burial: "What has happened to Cyndy?" As Christians we knew she would be welcomed into HEAVEN because she was an innocent child; apparently not everyone thinks so. No, some feel that if you do not profess Christ as your Savior verbally or by writing then you are not saved. I don't understand that, since if God knows what is in your heart what does it matter?

Anne turned to the scriptures; the Bible seemed to have a scripture for most torments. When she asked for help writing the book I agreed enthusiastically feeling my only input would be regarding medical explanations. However the question I thought we could answer quickly – what happened spiritually to Cyndy - proved to nag at us, particularly me, since it related to many of my patients that have passed on. The thought that if my patients couldn't acknowledge Christ in a traditional way they would be prevented from going to HEAVEN never occurred to me; on more than one occasion I would speculate how I would know them. Should I as a Christian believe that infants, premature babies, brain-injured children who could never understand Christian teachings, or that people never exposed to Christian teaching in their lifetime, are denied Paradise?

Since Anne and I both have obsessive compulsive disorder and different agendas for this book, it has taken a dozen years to finish. During that time medical science has evolved tremendously, attitudes in Christianity have changed, medications to treat OCD have improved, but some things haven't changed. Parents still bury their children, Christian beliefs are still fragmented by politicians and others, and despite our scientific achievements we are still left with the 3 questions of the ages: How did we get here? Where are we going? How long do we have? After you finish this book, you will know the answers for our little Cyndy; and hopefully acquire some knowledge, inspiration, and strength to find them for yourself.

The Alpha

The little angel looked up from the scene below him, closed his eyes briefly. Numbers, figures, and tallies flashed by like scores on an old video game in 3D until he had it all clear, in his mind, every one. He heard and felt the presence of the large angel above and behind him. "Have you got those numbers for me yet?"

"Yes sir," he replied. "Everything for this week: services, baptisms, communions, hosannas, hallelujahs, choirs, scripture readings, Bible study groups, readings, songs, hymns…everything that I keep track of. Are you ready for me to send?"

"Fire away, son." As the little angel concentrated, he could see the large form above him glow and convulse with energy. "Between you and the hundreds of other young angels keeping track of things, we can't afford to dally. So, as far as English-speaking hymns, 'Blessed Assurance' is still number one, is it? It has been for awhile, now, and it's improving worldwide. That means our girl CurlyTop is still at it."

He suppressed a smile, although he clearly felt it.

"Excuse me sir? CurlyTop?" whispered the little angel.

"She is a young angel like you, her given name Cyndy, with a Y. It is because of her that hymn is so popular. She never read the Bible or sang a note, but in her short time on earth she made an impression; when her mom and her doctor wrote a book about it, it touched a lot of hearts."

"Wow," said the little angel, looking a little forlorn. He was great with numbers and special, but letters and words in this unearthly plane gave him trouble.

He liked this place and the job kept him busy, but he couldn't remember the simplest of things except numbers…and he missed his mom.

"Would you like to get to know her as the rest of the world is?" The big angel cast a knowing glance at his young charge. "I can help you with the words, and in fact I will throw in something extra to help you."

The small angel nodded. "Close your eyes and prepare to receive, then," the large framed angel cautioned.

As the little angel relaxed, floods of words, blurred at first, then sharp and bright, began to roll upward like an old movie, each one caressed by his loving mother's soft purring voice.

Now it was his turn to smile, even though he was crying.

"On with the show."

ANNE H. HARRELL & LARRY E. WHITE, M.D.

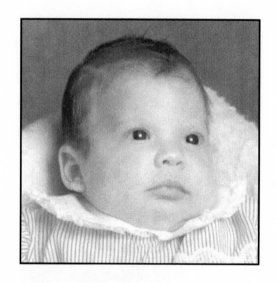

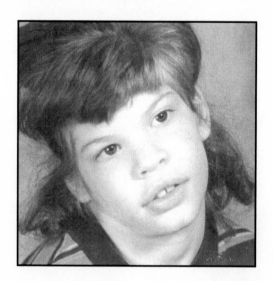

CHAPTER ONE

Blessed Assurance,
Jesus is Mine...

"Even though I walk through the valley of the shadow of death, I will fear no evil, for you are with me; your rod and your staff, they comfort me." - Psalm 23:4

New Year's morning 1997 seemed normal. Mark and I slept in. The children woke us eager to see the Rose Bowl parade and wanting breakfast. Katie and Joel had gotten up and come downstairs; Katie told us Cyndy was still sleeping. Mark made breakfast and began giving out medicine for the four of our five children who have physical and mental disabilities. Eleven year-old Cyndy still hadn't come downstairs. Katie wanted to play nurse and give Cyndy her meds since she was always an easy "patient" for her younger sister. She took the medicine that Mark measured out for Cyndy and ran back upstairs.

A few moments later she was back saying she couldn't get Cyndy to take her meds. Mark went up to wake her. Suddenly I heard him shouting "Cyndy is gone!" I wondered what he meant. Where is she? I ran upstairs and saw that she was still...her face was blue...ashen...

My first thought was to move her – to bring her downstairs and do CPR. I leaned over to give her four quick breaths. An odor escaped from her mouth. Her arms and hands were in mid-body position as they would be in mid-seizure. I tried to move them down to her side, only to realize they were stiff. My mind was racing...no heart beat! Not breathing! No this can't be happening to me! My daughter Help! Help! My baby is gone! No this can't have happened! No God No!

As I tried doing CPR once again I heard a voice. "Leave her alone now, she is Mine! She is healed now."

In a moment I felt a strong grip on my wrists, as if Cyndy had grabbed them, something she used to do when she wanted me to clap my hands together playing patty-cake with her. Patty-cake was Cyndy's way to let us and her doctors along with others know she was okay after a seizure. The more I tried to stop her from clapping my hands I couldn't. Then a peace came over me beyond my understanding. I knew that Cyndy was okay. As I got up off the floor, I knew that Cyndy would never seizure again! Cyndy was healed. Cyndy can walk and talk now and forever. I knew that Cyndy was gone to a much better place.

In a matter of minutes, my house was full of cops, firemen, paramedics, neighbors, church family, police chaplains, and social services. Questions were being fired at me left and right.

"Why did you move her out of her bed?"

"Why is your house in such a mess?"

"What do you have to say for living in conditions like this?"

My head was spinning. What was happening? Panic rose in my throat.

"Don't cover my daughter's face."

"She's not dead!" "I want my little girl back."

"Please God let me wake up, this is just part of a nightmare."

"Please GOD!"

CHAPTER TWO

Heir of Salvation

"Trust in the Lord with all your heart, and do not lean on your own understanding. In all your ways acknowledge him, and he will make straight your paths." - *Proverbs 3:5-6*

My childhood was not easy. I was born in Petersburg, Virginia in 1961 and raised in nearby Waverly. I was one of four children, sandwiched in between my older brother Jimmy and my younger sisters Mary and Cathy. By the age of five, I had endured several traumas including abuse, and witnessing a terrible accident where my brother was nearly killed by a tractor lawn mower.

Like everybody in my generation I was exposed to death of young children when I was growing up. Children died because of accidents or illnesses. I remember one extended family member – a child I played with – seemingly disappeared out of my life. When I asked about her, death was not discussed. It wasn't until years later when I was told. Somehow, I already knew.

Looking back though I can see how the Lord was working on me from a young age. My maternal grandparents faithfully took me to church when I was a child. Granny and Granddaddy would pray for my siblings and me. I remember Granny on her knees praying before

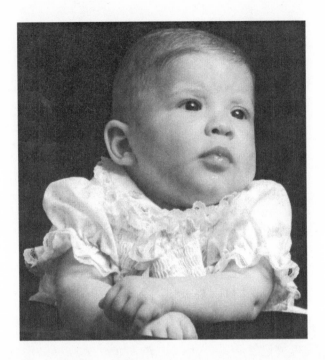

she would go to sleep at night. She would read to us from the Bible. Our bedtime stories were often from God's Word, usually a Psalm and something from the New Testament.

I remember being with Granddaddy when he died, and I still recall that he saw a bright light just before he went. Granny had on a dull light over the kitchen stove, while she was fixing him some coffee when he told her to cut off that bright light. I knew later that day my grandfather had seen the Lord coming for him. What a beautiful testament to Christ!

During my teenage years – when I should have been becoming a mature young lady - things were not well. I was scarred with battle wounds from the abuse I had endured as a young child. I was raped and ended up pregnant at the age of 14. I never felt like a normal child or teenager. I was labeled 'emotionally disturbed' as I wrestled with trying to come to terms with being raped. That label followed me for a long time. I tried to take my life several times before I finished school but even that didn't seem worth the trouble.

In February of 1983, I was talking to an old boyfriend Jeff. We had remained friends and I felt comfortable talking with him. I had begun thinking again about wanting to die. The burdens of sin, worry, and failed expectations weighed heavily on me. Jeff stopped me cold. Suddenly he told me in an authoritative voice, "you know what you need Anne is Christ in your life." Jeff tried to calm me down enough so that I could see the future I could have with the hope and light of Christ. He wanted me to be released from the ball and chain of sin, worry, and failed expectations from my past. At first I wanted to fight him. But patiently Jeff began to give me reasons why I needed Christ as my Savior. I realized that Jeff was demanding that I stop fighting and listen to him; I had struggled long enough. I was tired and ready to listen. As he told me about Jesus it was music to my ears. In my darkest moments, I found myself wanting to know more about Jesus – about this God that could take my emotional hurts and cast them into the deepest ocean, freeing me from the chains that bound me.

I have to admit that at first I thought that Jeff was "flying high." I couldn't believe what I was hearing him tell me. Several times I would take the phone from my ear, while looking at the phone shaking my head, I had kidded Jeff about what weed or booze he had been into that night. Jeff quickly snapped back telling me "I haven't been drinking or smoking weed." He explained "Anne, I want you to have the peace that I have should you were to die tonight you would be with Jesus. No one promises you another day Anne."

The gospel was like music to my ears. I could feel Christ knocking softly at the door of my heart. I could hear Christ telling me that if I opened the door He would come in and He will take the weights off my shoulders...the ball and chain would fall off instantly once I opened the door for Him to come in.

"Behold, I stand at the door and knock. If anyone hears my voice and opens the door, I will come in to him and eat with him, and he with me." - Rev. 3:20

"Take my yoke upon you, and learn from me, for I am gentle and lowly in heart, and you will find rest for your souls. For my yoke is easy, and my burden is light." - Matthew 11:29-30

Before the night was over Jeff had led me in the prayer of salvation. The weight fell from my shoulders – I wasn't bound anymore! Praise God! For the first time I could stand up straight and smile – truly smile. Joy had filled my heart.

After receiving Christ I immediately started praying that I would

Anne, Mark and Cyndy at her baptism.

find a loving husband; a husband who would love me and take away the horrendous unhappiness and pain of my past. I desperately wanted someone who would protect me from any further harm. I had carried the secret of my past abuse alone.

All I wanted after coming to know Christ was a man who would not look down on me; someone who would love me just for being Anne. I never dreamed that Christ would answer my prayers so quickly!

Within a month of my salvation conversation with Jeff I was blessed to meet my soul mate, the joy of my life, my beloved husband, Mark. The night when I gave my life to Christ I prayed that the Lord would send me a Christian man to be my husband but in fact the Lord had already the man in mind for me. He had been preparing Mark to come into my life and take on a huge job that will be never-ending until He calls Mark home! Mark had been saying the same prayer; he was looking for a woman who would crave his love and who would love him for he is.

Mark and I met through a dating service that some nurses I worked with dared me to join. We first talked by phone on March 1, 1983. Our phone calls would last anywhere from an hour to four or five hours. There was no question whether or not we loved each other when we finally met in person just five short days later. We had already fallen in love with one another's heart. We had looked deeply on the interior before we saw the exterior. When we were together for the first time on March 6 we certainly felt sparks fly! Our love for one another made it very hard to separate when our first date ended.

We quickly got engaged on March 19 just thirteen days after we first met. We set our wedding for June 10, 1983 but after some thought we decided to marry on April 23, 1983. Wow! We met, fell in love, and married all within six weeks time!

The Lord knew that I truly needed Mark in my life to help me grow into a more spiritually mature young woman. When Christ had put Mark into my life, He knew that Mark would love me for whom I am and not care about the past. After first meeting Mark I would break down and tell him little by little about my childhood. At first I feared that he would flee and not want me anymore. The more comfortable I got with Mark, the more I would tell him of my past. At times he would be moved to tears after hearing what had happened to me. Mark just wanted to take care of me; he did not care about the past. He just wanted to make sure that I would be taken care of now and in the future.

Mark had become a Christian several years before we met. He had come to know Christ in high school after he nearly died from a spider bite. Mark realized very quickly that none of us are promised a long life. He immediately understood the urgency of having Christ in his life.

Since Mark is eight years older than me by the time we met he was ready to settle down and have a family of his own. However all I knew was that I wanted a Christian man, one who would truly love me for who I was and nothing else. Mark took me under his wing, in a loving and caring way, and showed me the essential need to become stronger in my new walk with Christ. Being such a young Christian I had a lot to learn about knowing God as my Heavenly Father along with trusting Him as my Lord. I was not sure if I was ready for this religion thing or not at first, but it was high time for me to find out just who this God is and turn my life over to Him and trust Him whole-heartedly with my well being.

Mark had no clue what he had gotten himself into but committed to stick with me through thick and thin. Unfortunately my childish ways often stood in the way of Mark and I being happily married at first. We had countless adjustments to make our first year of marriage. We both brought some heavy emotional baggage into the relationship that neither of us had dealt with before we were married. We did not have the energy or the patience to work through our problems on our own. That baggage proved to be very destructive to our relationship.

To be honest, we fought violently all the time early on in our marriage. A neighbor who lived a couple houses down from us would witness Mark being locked out of our home after an argument. Mark would have to plead with me to let him back in the house. I was just so very high strung and unreachable. At times, I was incredibly stubborn and hostile and unwilling to compromise with Mark. We never took the crucial time we needed to really get to know each other or love each other as we should have. We never met in the middle to settle our differences. There was little trust and dependence between us.

Mark, Anne, Cyndy and Mark Jr.

Looking back we can both see how we were brought closer to God and one another because we had to depend on Him. Money was a frequent cause of stress and source of disagreements between us. I remember clearly our second month's rent on our apartment was due and we didn't have enough to make it. Work on the waterfront was slow even with my father-in-law – Williams Wesley Harrell, Sr., (whom I called "Dad") –getting Mark work on the same pier whenever he could. We witnessed the hand of God just when we needed it the most. Mark had a four-hour ship job that lasted all week. Every day that week it rained on and off causing the men to be sent home at noon. No matter how many hours Mark worked, whether it was four or six hours, he was paid for eight hours and then anything more was counted as overtime. We had more than enough money for the rent!

It was a year of learning for Mark and me. It was a time for me to stop running from my problems and learn to deal with them head on. The Lord wanted me to find peace in His Word, where fear gives way to trust, and trust becomes faith. My faith grew as I learned that the Lord will walk with us in our darkest moments and that there is solace in the Lord. Mark was willing to stand beside me. He helped me work through my emotional problems and learn to enjoy our marriage.

Looking back on the beginning of our marriage, I realize that I did not trust God as my Father or really recognize His loving character. I could not understand how a loving father could love an emotionally unstable woman like me, and I did not believe that God saw me as His own precious child. I just wanted Him to bless me and I felt that He was being callous or unreasonable when things did not work in my best interest! If it was not done my way I would throw a fit. Nevertheless, because God refused to let me go, He worked in my life to showed me His eternal, unconditional love. God used such extreme circumstances to get my complete attention and change my attitude and lifestyle eternally for good. Because God loves me, He will go to great lengths to draw me near.

Learning to love God and be able to accept His love was very tough. He showed me that I was His daughter and my life did matter to Him.

He definitely wanted to be part of my life and bless me with magnificent, eternal treasures. I have heartfelt thanks for Jeff who cared about my soul back in February of 1983. My marriage to Mark must have been made in Heaven because as I am writing we are working on our 27th year together!

Over these 28 years we have made many beautiful memories as well as some that have brought on sorrow. Yet if I had it to do over again I would not trade one second because of the love, strength, and growth we have had in Christ. The painful memories have taught us how to love each other as Christ loves us; pain has bonded us together instead of pulling us apart. By our first Christmas together, we experienced enormous joy - we found out that we were expecting our first child who was due that summer.

Our first child, Mark Harrell Jr. entered our lives on August 24, 1984. Our first daughter Cyndy was born just 14 months later on October 30, 1985. Little did we know how that little baby girl would change our lives.

> Prayer:
> Thank you, Lord, for taking hold of our lives and holding us in your arms. You were faithful to us from the very beginning of our marriage, and You guided us with Your hand through the joys and troubles in our life. Teach us to continue to put our trust in You and depend on You alone.
> In Christ,
> Amen

CHAPTER THREE

A Special Angel is Born

"Behold, children are a heritage from the Lord, the fruit of the womb a reward. Like arrows in the hand of a warrior are the children of one's youth. Blessed is the man who fills his quiver with them! He shall not be put to shame when he speaks with his enemies in the gate."
- Psalm 127:3-5

When I first found out that I was pregnant with Cyndy I was actually expecting twins. I had no idea that there were two fetuses until I was 10 weeks along. Just when Mark and I were taking in the surprise of a twin pregnancy the first signs of complications started. I began to bleed and went to see my OB/GYN; he did an ultrasound and saw two egg sacs but he didn't see the babies' heartbeats at first in either one. The doctor was sure that I had probably miscarried both babies. He was about to perform the D&C and did one more ultrasound just to see if any viable fetal tissue remained before the surgery. He and the nurses were surprised to see Cyndy's little heart beating ever so strong! It caused him to send me home and put me on complete bedrest until the bleeding had completely stopped. This was absolutely the hand of God. Had the doctor not checked one last time before surgery we would not have known Cyndy was waiting to be born. Although we were greatly saddened by the sudden loss of one of our babies, we were thankful for the one remaining. We looked forward to the birth of the other baby, our dearest Cyndy.

When I went into labor with Cyndy it was a cool fall crisp sunny day. I had a list of 50 things to do before I could lay my head down to sleep that night. I had been feeling somewhat achy but really didn't think much of it with all that I had to do. Labor didn't cross my mind as I wasn't due until December. I went about my daily chores, but as the day went on the pain in my back and lower stomach started to feel worse. I kept going, making refreshments for the Pioneer Girls

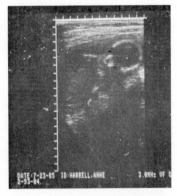

"I almost didn't happen."

Club meeting at church that evening; I had promised to make cupcakes and bring the punch. I wasn't going to let the girls down!

But the pain in my lower back was increasing and my stomach muscles were tightening. My Mom called me from work to check up on me. While on the phone, I noticed those stabbing and squeezing pains were coming like clockwork. I said something to my mom about the pain and without telling me she began timing my contractions while we were talking. When she realized that I was having contractions every five minutes she told me I was in labor. I told her that I couldn't be! She was worried that I had gone into premature labor.

I was in denial but after I realized that I was in active labor, Mom insisted that I call the doctor and tell him about my recurring premature labor pains. I quickly realized there was no time to play around; I needed to get in gear now that I knew was going to have that baby today. Suddenly I remembered the struggle of labor and delivery pain when I had Cyndy's older brother Mark. OH NO...PANIC! I grabbed the phone and called my husband - big Mark - at work. In a piercing, high-pitched voice I told him I was going into actual labor...I AM HAVING THIS BABY NOW!

Mark went to pieces. He had no means to travel to the hospital since we had only one car and I had driven him to work earlier in the day. When I told him that I was going to drive to pick him up – while I was in active labor! - he had a fit. There was no way that he was going to let me drive to the hospital knowing that I would be putting myself, the baby, and little Mark in danger. I had no choice but to call 911 for the ambulance and tell them I was ready to give birth any minute and needed to be taken to the hospital. My poor little Mark wasn't sure

Our newborn angel.

what was going on when the ambulance arrived. Thankfully while little Mark and I were on the way to the hospital my father-in-law was on his way to the port to get Mark.

Strapped to the stretcher, with the sirens blaring and the ambulance speeding and then slamming on brakes, I arrived at Norfolk General Hospital in active labor, sore, and with a serious headache. Little Mark Jr. was crying "Mama" over and over and had the most pitiful look on his face. He was anxiously reaching for me with both hands just pleading for me to take him. The tears stopped when the emergency technicians placed him on the stretcher beside me to go to the Labor and Delivery Unit. For a one year old this was very cool! I will never forget the surprised expression on little Mark's skeptical face when my water broke. He gave me the funniest look as if to say "why did you go and wet the bed and me?!" Once in the room, he kept trying to hop off the bed every time the nurses turned their backs. I felt helpless not being able to help the nurses, while he gave them a run for their money and refused to stay on the bed with me any longer.

While they were rushing to prepare me for Cyndy's delivery Mark Sr. and my father-in-law arrived. The nurses begged for one of them to take little Mark home. Just before Dad took Mark Jr. home with him the OB/GYN came in to give me the epidural without considering that it would embarrass my father-in-law. The nurses and doctor quickly began to prepare me and poor Dad saw more of me than he bargained for! I screamed for Dad to hold my hand but he was so uncomfortable that he wanted to get as far away as possible from the room!

Once the doctors determined that Cyndy was in a breach position, they had to turn her for delivery. The doctor thought that after turning her it would still take a while before she would be born. However Cyndy had other ideas. By the time Mark returned to the room I was already pushing. Because the epidural had already taken effect I didn't feel any pain, just some pressure. I didn't realize that Cyndy was getting impatient and wanted out! My nurse, Terri, had set up mirrors so I could watch the beautiful miracle of Cyndy coming into this awesome world. With Mark by my side it was time for Cyndy to be born, as if she felt like I was stopping her from coming before Mark returned!

Cyndy arrived at 5:59 p.m. on Wednesday, October 30, 1985, six weeks premature. She weighed in at six pounds and was 18 ¼ inches long. The birth was traumatic for her. In addition to being in the breach position the umbilical cord was wrapped around her neck and her heart was abnormally enlarged which resulted in breathing complications immediately after delivery. My heart begun to pound hard when I realized that Cyndy had a

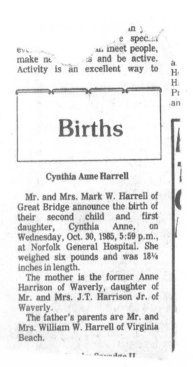

in
e spec...
ev... a... meet people,
make ne ...s and be active.
Activity is an excellent way to

Births

Cynthia Anne Harrell

Mr. and Mrs. Mark W. Harrell of Great Bridge announce the birth of their second child and first daughter, Cynthia Anne, on Wednesday, Oct. 30, 1985, 5:59 p.m., at Norfolk General Hospital. She weighed six pounds and was 18¼ inches in length.

The mother is the former Anne Harrison of Waverly, daughter of Mr. and Mrs. J.T. Harrison Jr. of Waverly.

The father's parents are Mr. and Mrs. William W. Harrell of Virginia Beach.

blue tinge to her. I began to think that she may not have made it since I didn't hear her cry. The nurses whisked her off to the neonatal intensive care unit (NICU) nursery to stabilize her.

When I saw her later that evening, I couldn't believe how beautiful she was. She had a head full of gorgeous, curly, dirty blonde hair; her big blue sparkling eyes spoke volumes. Cyndy spent her first few weeks of life in the NICU nursery, fighting for her life. As a preemie she had jaundice (which is common for premature babies) but also numerous problems including an enlarged heart. When we visited her poor little body was stuck with several IVs and covered with wires hooked to numerous monitors. With so much medical equipment we were afraid that we would hurt her or accidentally pull something out when we went to hold and touch her. Lying in the incubator she looked so helpless and fragile. Our hearts broke when we saw her but we were also overjoyed that we had a daughter now! Throughout the day, from morning to night, we kept praying for the Lord to please take care of our newborn daughter. We knew that long, shaky days lay ahead.

It was depressing knowing that we could only hold her for a few minutes, just long enough to feed her. The longest and most painful days were when we couldn't take her out of the incubator. All we could do was reach inside the clear plastic bed and touch her petite little body. I would cry that I couldn't hold her against my chest and comfort her when the nurses and doctors were poking and prodding her. My biggest desire was to take her home and be a mother to her. I wanted to hold and feed my baby girl and not have to worry about nurses telling me when or if I could hold her. She was MY baby girl! Honestly there were times that I wished the nurses would fall off the face of the earth. Every opportunity that we could get to hold our precious little newborn daughter we did, even if it meant going to the hospital late at night.

Cyndy had an angelic look to her. Anyone that saw her thought she was the most beautiful baby. There was one nurse that was so taken with Cyndy that she began acting like she was her baby. No matter what I said or did, she didn't want me to touch Cyndy. One day it got so bothersome that when Dr. Garrison came by the nursery to check on Cyndy, he found me crying because I wanted to hold my baby and the nurse had taken her from me. Dr. Garrison was quick to tell the nurses to let me hold her when I wanted, but when we finally did hold her, it was only for about five minutes at a time. We never wanted to put her down. When the nurses demanded that she be put back under the bright bilirubin lights our hearts felt heavy. The postpartum blues got the worst of me during the two weeks she was in the NICU. All I wanted to do was cry and be with my baby.

While she was in the hospital we stayed on our knees praying that God would strengthen Cyndy's little body, pleading "please God let her get better and come home quickly." There were times when we weren't sure what or how to pray for Cyndy or even for our family, yet the Holy Spirit knew just what to pray and when to pray.

> "Likewise the Spirit helps us in our weakness. For we do not know what to pray for as we ought, but the Spirit himself intercedes for us with groanings too deep for words. And he who searches hearts knows what is the mind of the Spirit, because the Spirit intercedes for the saints according to the will of God. And we know that for those who love God all things work together for good, for those who are called according to his purpose." - Romans 8:26-28

Having a sick premature newborn proved to be trying not only for our faith but also for our marriage. We had to rely on God alone to get us through each and every day. We felt down and tired from running sun up until sundown. However, God gave us the emotional and physi-

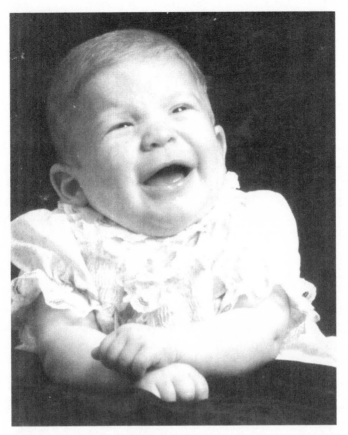

Should I laugh or cry?

cal strength we needed to deal with her sickness while she was in the NICU and He helped us to care for her once she was home. We praised God for the precious little girl that He had placed in our charge until He would reclaim her for His glory.

We were thankful God chose us to raise His special daughter because ultimately she was His child, just on loan to us. We were just the stewards of His child, and our job was to see that she was raised well in a Christian home, which we did our best to try and do.

In spite of her ongoing medical problems, we loved having our baby girl home. We loved watching her meet milestones, and could see the blessings the Lord had in store for us. Cyndy's blonde curls turned dark brown that curled like a coiled spring. Her blue eyes were irresistible. She was a very friendly baby with an angelic smile. We could see the Lord had sent her here not only for our joy and happiness but for others' happiness too. I remember being at the mall with Cyndy in a carrier against my chest. She was so petite and angelic looking that she drew crowds. People just had to see her and ask if she was real.

Mark recalls first meeting his sweet daughter Cyndy:

"The most pleasurable opportunity to hold our second baby, our first daughter Cynthia Anne Harrell, was a feeling that nobody could imagine but a father with his new daughter. There was an instant bond. The thought that THIS was my daughter that Anne and I had made! As I looked in her eyes I could see all the love Cyndy had in her. God took the unconditional love between Him and us, and rolled it into a very pretty girl who was His servant and our daughter."

Cyndy was just a tiny bundle, a miracle of life, God's creation, and a little person with her whole life ahead of her. I dreamed about baking cookies with her, sewing clothes, and doing all the typical mother-daughter things including helping her plan her wedding and being there for her when she had her first child. Dressing her up in frilly dresses, making her look dainty as a princess, gave us glimpses of the beautiful young woman that she would one day become. Mark Sr. talked about anticipating the joy of having the rest of his life to protect, hold, love, and see Cyndy grow up into a woman.

Over the first several weeks at home Cyndy began filling out and becoming a little butterball! I could see all the wonders of the blessings that were bestowed on me as a mother. Cyndy's smiles and coos brought joy to this mother's heart; watching her grow I began to understand how much my Heavenly Father must love me. I will never forget her first belly laugh or how her sparkly eyes lit up when she saw my sister Cathy's doll. Cathy would tease her with the doll just to hear her big belly laugh, yet when Cathy would walk away Cyndy would start to cry so of course, Cathy had to come back to play some more.

By the time Cyndy was two months old, she no longer wanted to sleep all the time. She kept my days very busy! She didn't want to be in the crib in her room - she was a people person and wanted to be the center of attention where she could see everything going on. She did not like to lie on her back. If I laid her down on the carpet in our living room she would constantly roll over on her belly and push up on her arms or she would start rolling and make her way into another room. If

I had only known I would have 11 short years with her, oh how I would have done things differently! To me Cyndy seemed like a normal happy-go-lucky baby and I treated her as such. I never dreamed that we would endure the hardships of her seizures, much less losing her to death at a young age.

A cherished letter that I wrote to Cyndy on November 13, 1985:

> Dear Cyndy,
> As I write this letter, you have turned two weeks old today. God sure answered my prayers when He gave me you. You sure have been a blessing to me. I cannot wait until you are old enough for me to bake cookies with you at Christmas and teach you how to sew. Cyndy, you and your mother are going to have a great time.
> Love,
> Your mom

As parents we don't always realize that we are simply stewards of God's children; they do not belong to us, but to Him. The Bible tells us children are just on loan to us, and therefore God has every right to receive them unto Himself in His perfect timing. Psalm 127:3 says "Behold, children are a heritage from the Lord; the fruit of the womb is a reward." It is easy to forget that our children belong to God when they are called home at an early age. It hurts to surrender them back to the God who is the Lord and Creator of everything. In His mercy and kindness, God graciously gives us a very special gift through our children, and for that we give Him eternal thanks.

> Prayer:
> Thank you, Lord, for our children. Please help us to remember that you generously provided the special gift of a newborn baby as an undeserved gift and blessing from heaven above. Help us remember that in Your goodness You can take our children at any time and we must enjoy them while we can, knowing that any day could be our last day with them. Give us the grace to trust in the perfection of Your plan for our life and theirs. Teach us the true faith of a child that we might walk more closely to You.
> In Christ,
> Amen

CHAPTER FOUR

On Our Knees Praying Through Early Emergencies

"You are my hiding place; you will protect me from trouble and surround me with songs of deliverance." - Psalm 32:7

After leaving the NICU Cyndy seemed healthy. There were no clues that Cyndy's health was changing rapidly until a week after she turned six months old. In the early dawn hours of one morning in May 1986, Mark and I were awakened by a blood-curdling scream. We assumed it was just Cyndy hungry and crying but when we tried to pacify her with a bottle she stopped crying for only a moment. Her screaming quickly persisted and became worse. Cyndy's eyes showed pure terror. Then, with a blank stare and no warning she began gasping for air. Cyndy's face had a bluish tinge and the color instantly deepened to a purplish bluish tint. Abruptly she went limp and then immediately her small body began violently convulsing.

When the paramedics arrived, they sized up Cyndy's apparent medical condition and made it unmistakably clear that her condition was grave. They explained respectfully but directly that Cyndy might not live through the night. Can you imagine hearing someone tell you those very words about your own precious baby? Hearing the paramedics warn us that Cyndy might not even make it to the hospital, I cried

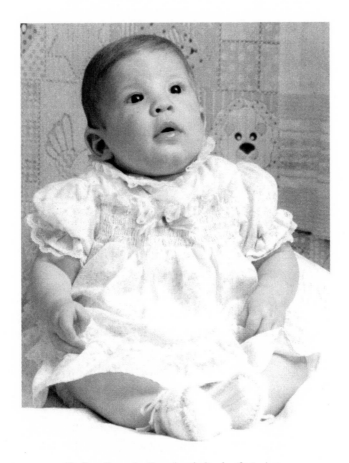

Cyndy at 6 months, three days before her first seizure.

out to God, "LORD, PLEASE SAVE MY BABY, PLEASE DON'T LET HER DIE"!

In my agony, I cried out to the great Physician, the God over every cell in Cyndy's body, the Lord who preserves our souls from danger. I called out to the only One who could help, realizing it requires a dire circumstance to remind us that we are not in control and that only God is sufficient to meet our most heartfelt needs. What a humbling experience - to watch the almighty hand of God work in such a serious and sobering situation. When Cyndy's condition worsened we were forced to make a choice: stop at Chesapeake General Hospital to stabilize Cyndy or continue on to Norfolk General Hospital.

That was one of those once-in-a-lifetime significant moments. We knew without a doubt that God was truly with us in our darkest hour.

Our little "center of attention."

My desperate prayer was on the verge of being answered as the ambulance turned into the Chesapeake General Hospital's ER entrance. I felt an enormous calmness sweep over me; I had His peaceful assurance that Cyndy was going to be okay. The sensation was exactly like God putting His arms around me and holding me tightly while giving me the perfect blessed assurance that Cyndy was not going to die. No one was actually touching me yet my Lord was holding me and encouraging me that He was in control and He would never leave me or forsake me. I knew that He was promising to take absolute care of my daughter. God was calling me to trust Him and surrender to Him and His love completely enveloped me. In the middle of my fear suddenly I knew there was nothing to fear anymore. I knew the Holy Spirit was speaking to me while He was holding me. I felt absolute peace of mind in the eye of the storm. It was a feeling I still can't explain.

My mothers' instinct was to fall to pieces when I realized that Cyndy was going to require more nurturing and medical care than a normal baby would require. I was not sure if we could give her the special care that she required. I had been trained in some nursing skills—CPR and additional EMT training —but I never thought I would need to use it on a family member, especially on my own child. I kept asking myself: could I remain calm when an emergency occurred? Would I be able to do what is medically necessary for my own daughter when she was in crisis?

All of these "what if" questions were answered when it came time to give Cyndy the emergency medical care needed. I did what I had to do for her even though I would lose it emotionally after the fact. At times Cyndy's medical problems were too extensive for us to deal with on our own. We had to rely on the Lord to deal with each emergency as they happened. We found ourselves praying and pleading to the Lord for much-needed wisdom and strength to take care of Cyndy with each new day.

When we are going through trials in our lives that are devastating the Lord wants us as in Psalm 119:145 where the psalmist says,

"I cry out with my whole heart. Hear me, O Lord."

Our loving Father always hears our prayers and answers them according to His perfect plan. In John 14:13-14 Jesus says,

"And whatever you ask in My name, that I will do, that the Father may be glorified in the Son. If you ask anything in my name, I will do it."

Of course, a selfish understanding of these verses would lead us to believe that God does what we tell Him to do. Because of His perfect goodness and mercy, God's plan is always right, even if it does not match our own wishes. His desires and thoughts are higher than ours are, and we will only know true joy if we surrender to Him.

I can still picture in my mind that precious little baby, our daughter Cyndy, in the ER after they had placed her on the ventilator to help her breathe. I can still feel the pain that went through me as I watched in horror. The ER doctor worked diligently to give her the urgent care that she needed to help stop the life-threatening seizures. A peace beyond understanding came over me while the doctors worked meticulously to stabilize her before transferring her to Norfolk General Hospital.

While at Norfolk General Hospital my heart was breaking seeing her tiny, helpless figure laying on the gurney. She was on the ventilator trying to cry out for help but there was no sound coming from her. To see her breathing easier, even though the machine was doing it for her, helped me to breathe easier. In the midst of our emotional storm we were also having a severe electrical storm. Even though it was night-time in my mind, I could see the refection of a bright rainbow over the horizon. I knew that everything was going to be all right.

Within a few short hours of Cyndy being ventilated and sent to the Pediatric Intensive Care Unit (PICU) she managed to come off the respirator. She began breathing on her own and moved to the Progressive

Care Unit (PCU). Before I could see Cyndy I was questioned by doctors, nurses, and social workers about what happened with Cyndy earlier in the day that could cause her to seizure. I think they suspected I may have shaken her. I was not happy about what they were asking me, yet I knew that all possibilities had to be ruled out for Cyndy's sake. Prayers were all that sustained

Happy times punctuated by sudden illness.

me. The Lord was gracious enough to show me that He had heard my prayers Cyndy was going to be all right, which was a huge relief! Looking back, I can honestly say that I would not have wanted to be any other place than in the arms of God during my darkest hours.

Every time Cyndy would have a seizure we discovered she had a high fever or an ear infection. The doctors thought those conditions triggered the seizures, even though there were other underlying issues which were actually causing them. None of us knew this was just the beginning of Cyndy's declining health. We didn't know the near future held much uncertainty and that more health problems would plague Cyndy during her short life.

Within two months after the first seizure, we ended up in the hospital again. On a humid July morning, I had put Cyndy down for a nap after she had eaten breakfast and been bathed. Prompted by the Lord to go check on Cyndy, I found her near-lifeless body lying in her crib. When I called the paramedics I was so traumatized I couldn't even tell the dispatcher where I had laid Cyndy down.

A paramedic named Sean who had been on duty when Cyndy had her first seizure came running over to help when he heard that Cyndy was not breathing. He was able to quiet me down enough for me to tell him where I had laid Cyndy down. By the time the ambulance arrived, Sean had already gotten Cyndy breathing again and had put an IV in her arm to give her valium to stop the seizures. Once again, after stabilizing

Cyndy at Chesapeake General Hospital they transported her to CHKD for evaluation and further treatment. Once again she got better. Once again, fever seemed to be the cause. And once again, we were afraid.

Our lifestyle changed and became centered on being prepared for Cyndy's health needs. Every time she would experience a seizure we knew to call the paramedics. We put 911 on speed dial so I didn't have to worry about being so stressed from Cyndy's scary seizures when my mind would draw a blank. We got to the point where we felt like we were living in constant crises mode all the time. Mark and I had no time to ourselves. Even so, being in urgent situations kept us close to the Lord and clinging to each other.

There were times when our precious little girl was so sick, it seemed like the hands on the clock were standing still while we waited for the emergency crew to arrive. I lived in constant fear she would die right before my eyes in the five to ten minutes it took for the rescue squad to get to us. When they came I would worry if they would they get her to the hospital in time to save her life. Internally I was screaming "PLEASE GOD HELP CYNDY, PLEASE GOD DON'T LET HER DIE, WHY ISN'T THE EMERGENCY CREW GETTING HERE?" "HELP ME GOD!"

The day before Thanksgiving in 1986, Cyndy spiked a high fever and began having seizures again, only this time they were worse than usual. They would stop and then, usually in an hour or less, happen again. I called Dr. Forrest White – Cyndy's pediatrician and no relation to Dr. Larry White – and he elected to treat her in the office. He watched her and treated her with injections of Phenobarbital. I was in constant prayer that she would stop having these awful convulsions, and that the medicine would work. By mid-afternoon her seizures had stopped, and we left Dr. White's office. Since there was no time to go home before picking up Mark from work, we went down to the pier to stay with my father-in-law. For a couple of hours things were blessedly quiet. But after picking up Mark, Cyndy's seizures started again, and I was frantic.

It seemed like we were going to lose our year-old baby girl right then. My thoughts turned to God. Where was He when Cyndy was having one seizure after another? Did He even care that she was so sick? Why was the Lord allowing this to happen when Christmas was just a month away?

Heading home Cyndy's condition grew more serious. She began to turn blue and was having problems breathing. We rushed Cyndy to the nearest hospital where Jay, a friend from our church, was the ER doctor on duty. Jay recognized my screams and came running from back in the ER to take Cyndy from me. He rapidly examined her and then put her on a ventilator and administered medicine to stop the seizures. After stabilizing Cyndy, Jay sent her to the children's hospital for further stabilization and care. Even though we ended up eating turkey at the hospital that year we were simply thankful that Cyndy was alive.

Our Heavenly Father knew that no matter what we saw happening He was going to be with her through each one of the crises. He knew what He was doing with her even when we could not see His plan. Cyndy was at peace with her Heavenly Father even when we were not at peace with Him. We had to learn to lean completely on Christ to get us through every seizure. We knew there was going to come a time when Christ would call Cyndy home we just didn't know when the day would come.

During her health emergencies we were getting glimpses of God's intentions for Cyndy's life. The Lord Almighty purposefully created her to be an exceptional child of His to further His Kingdom. She was meant to be a little girl with special needs and to glorify God by showing her Christ-like love to everyone she encountered while here on earth. That day before Thanksgiving in 1986 was our introduction to 11 years of laughter, tears, joy, and sorrow. God was forming in us a greater dependence on His grace. We had to trust God with our precious little girl because she was only on loan to us. Because Mark and I are normal, sinful human beings, this thought did not come easily. We did not even learn willingly about trusting in God, our faith and trust continues to be a huge challenge for all of us. Throughout Cyndy's life, we had to surrender – with our whole hearts – our little girl to the Lord, knowing that children in her condition are expected to return to their heavenly Father at a young age.

We began learning in this stormy season of our lives to just look up to our Heavenly Father and trust Him to be beside us every step of the way. We recalled Psalm 121:1-8:

> *"I lift up my eyes to the hills.*
> *From where does my help come?*
> *My help comes from the Lord,*
> *who made heaven and earth.*

He will not let your foot be moved;
he who keeps you will not slumber.
Behold, he who keeps Israel
will neither slumber nor sleep.

The Lord is your keeper;
the Lord is your shade on your right hand.
The sun shall not strike you by day,
nor the moon by night.

The Lord will keep you from all evil;
he will keep your life.
The Lord will keep
your going out and your coming in
from this time forth and forevermore."

God is our help and our comforter. If God is not on our side, who can be for us? He keeps us safe and secure. We can count on the Lord to help us through our rough times in life.

Prayer:
Thank you, Lord, for giving us the strength and wisdom to know Your will and everlasting love. Help us to continue to trust in Your goodness and mercy.
In Christ,
Amen

CHAPTER FIVE

As our Church Embraces Us

*"How good and pleasant it is when brothers live together in unity!
It is like precious oil poured on the head, running down on the beard,
running down on Aaron's beard, down upon the collar of his robes. It
is as if the dew of Hermon were falling on Mount Zion. For there the
LORD bestows his blessing, even life forevermore." - Psalm 133:1-3*

We prayed for a church home and God answered, leading us to Calvary Presbyterian Church in Norfolk, Virginia, in the early part of 1985. The late Pastor Leon Wardell headed the small church and right from the time we began attending Calvary, we made his job an exciting one! Just a few months after we joined the church Cyndy was born. Calvary embraced us – and Cyndy – continually and in so many practical ways. Pastor Wardell and the elders met and prayed for Mark and me when I went into premature labor with Cyndy that October night. They bathed us in prayer since Cyndy was a preemie with numerous health problems. They threw us a baby shower for Cyndy and we were overwhelmed by their generosity – a high chair, blankets, clothes, and gift cards. Calvary's entire congregation has such a strong love for the babies of the church; they were committed to generously assisting young parents like us in any and every way humanly possible. The church's strong love for all of its members is continually shown through prayer and providing for practical needs.

In her first year Cyndy started having seizures. Pastor Wardell kept a close eye on our family during services. If a deacon came to get Mark or myself because Cyndy had a seizure in the nursery Pastor Wardell would stop the service, pray for Cyndy right then, and give the congregation an opportunity to join in prayer for us before continuing.

But it wasn't just the Pastor and deacons who cared so well for us at Calvary. Mark and I were incredibly blessed by a couple in the

Easter Sunday after church.

congregation who worked as ER physicians. Doctors Jay and Kim Piland were eager to help us whenever and however they could to keep Cyndy from dying at a young age. If we were alerted during a service that Cyndy was having a seizure they would jump up and follow us to see if there was anything medically they could do to assist her. When Cyndy's seizures were happening more often and lasting longer Jay and Kim petitioned the elders to consider ways the church could help us access better health care. The church elders agreed to pay for us to see a specialist in Pennsylvania whom the Wardells knew. They were very concerned that she would die during a service. I remember a time at Calvary when Cyndy was in a prolonged seizure. It quickly became obvious that there was nothing more Jay could do for Cyndy without medical equipment. He physically scooped Cyndy up into his arms and headed for Sentara Leigh Hospital, just a half a mile away. Repeatedly the Pilands did whatever needed to be done to care for Cyndy, purely out of love.

When a financial need arose, someone at our church always seemed to step up and meet the need no matter how little or big it was. It was neat to see whose heart God would move in some way that would richly blessed our hearts. For example, in addition to making arrangements for us to go to a well-known neurosurgeon in Pennsylvania to see if there was anything that could be done for Cyndy and Mark Jr., who had begun to show developmental delays and signs of being handicapped, the church paid for the motel bill, for our food, and medical treatment for both our children. We saw Matthew 7:7-11 come to life at Calvary.

> *"Ask, and it will be given to you; seek, and you will find; knock, and it will be opened to you. For everyone who asks receives, and the one who seeks finds, and to the one who knocks it will be opened. Or which one of you, if his son asks him for bread, will give him a stone? Or if he asks for a fish, will give him a serpent? If you then, who are evil, know how to give good gifts to your children, how much more will your Father who is in heaven give good things to those who ask him!"*

Since we have been at Calvary two pastors have been there. When Pastor Wardell retired 1989, our church was without a pastor for a couple of years. We were blessed in late fall of 1990 with a new pastor, the Rev. Mark J. Bender who has been there since and has walked with us through numerous crises.

We have never gone without while we have been at Calvary. Pastors have spent many late nights caring for us at our home because of crises. Pastor Bender would encourage Calvary to pay for countless mortgage, phone, or power bills when we were in need. Several people from church gave us monetary gifts anonymously, so that they could not receive the credit. One Christmas we received gift certificates in the mail for the local mall for the kids. What an example of sacrificial love! God's mercy and provision have been shown through the generous giving of people at Calvary. Church members have given to us so generously, not only food for our bodies, but nourishment for our souls.

When we ask for something in Christ's name with true faith, we are assured that Christ WILL give us what we ask, as long as it is in His plan according to His riches in glory. God is so superior about providing our needs, no matter how huge or small, nothing is too immense or minute for God. This is what Jesus talks about in John 14:12-14:

> *"Truly, truly, I say to you, whoever believes in me will also do the works that I do; and greater works than these will he do, because I am going to the Father. Whatever you ask in my name, this I will do, that the Father may be glorified in the Son. If you ask me anything in my name, I will do it."*

I often had a difficult time trusting God to provide, yet our Lord is a loving Father who understands my weakness. My problem is that I look at the storm around me, and I do not keep my eyes on Christ. When the rain and wind is blowing I worry about being tossed around instead of being braced in the safe arms of Christ. Even one of Jesus' own disciples struggled with doubt, as recorded in John 20: 24-28:

> *"Now Thomas, one of the Twelve, called the Twin, was not with them when Jesus came. Therefore, the other disciples told him, 'We have seen the Lord.' But he said to them, 'Unless I see in his hands the mark of the nails, and place my finger into the mark of the nails, and place my hand into his side, I will never believe.' Eight days later, his disciples were inside again, and Thomas was with them. Although the doors were locked, Jesus came and stood among them and said, 'Peace be with you.' Then he said to Thomas, 'Put your finger here, and see my hands; and put out your hand, and place it in my side. Do not disbelieve, but believe.' Thomas answered him, 'My Lord and my God!' Jesus said to him, 'Have you believed because you have seen me? Blessed are those who have not seen and yet have believed.'"*

Christ was loving and merciful to Thomas. Jesus showed Thomas His glory despite his lack of faith so that Thomas could see and worship Christ. Aren't we all like Thomas at times?

God used so many people at Calvary to build my faith and encourage our family while they helped care for Cyndy. One of our deacons, Bill Tuck, let Cyndy walk with him while he did his ushering duties. That would make her so happy! We would hear her clapping her hands and cooing in the foyer. Bill recalled:

> "I would go get Cyndy out of the nursery and let her make rounds with me. I would take her outside and let her run or push her on the swing. She would coo and give me the biggest smiles. I liked that she did not care who you were she simply loved you for being you. She would give me kisses and wanted me to pick her up every time she saw me. As big as she got she still wanted me to pick her up. I got great joy out of taking her under my wing."

I remember walking by the nursery one Sunday and seeing a friend, John Leggore, in the rocking chair with Cyndy in his lap. She was resting her head on his shoulder, fast asleep. Seeing her resting peacefully on John's shoulder gave me great encouragement. We have been blessed by the women in the nursery who did not mind the extra attention a special child like Cyndy needed. Marge, Lavada, Jean, and Linda were among the many women who would take Cyndy in the nursery to give Mark and me a break at church. Sometimes, Cyndy would wear these women out, but they never minded watching after her. Pastor and Mrs. Wardell and Joanne would babysit for us when Mark Jr. had his surgeries, and they were always there for Cyndy when she was sick or in the hospital. What a blessing they had been to us!

> "Therefore I tell you, do not be anxious about your life, what you will eat, or what you will drink, nor about your body, what you will put on. Is not life more than food and the body more than clothing? Look at the birds of the air: they neither sow nor reap nor gather into barns, and yet your heavenly Father feeds them. Are you not of more value than they? And which of you by being anxious can add a single hour to his span of life? And why are you anxious about clothing? Consider the lilies of the field, how they grow: they neither toil nor spin, yet I tell you, even Solomon in all his glory was not arrayed like one of these. But if God so clothes the grass of the field, which today is alive and tomorrow is thrown into the oven, will he not much more clothe you, O you of little faith? Therefore do not be anxious, saying, 'What shall we eat?' or 'What shall we drink?' or 'What shall we wear?' For the Gentiles seek after all these things, and your heavenly Father knows that you need them all. But seek first the kingdom of God and his righteousness, and all these things will be added to you. Therefore, do not be anxious about tomorrow, for tomorrow will be anxious for itself. Sufficient for the day is its own trouble." - Matthew 6:25-34

God will look after my family no matter what happens to us. Christ will provide according to His will when we ask anything in His name. Our church sure has taken care of us!

Cyndy opened the door at Calvary to the handicapped and broke ground for others at Calvary who have handicaps or disorders. She challenged people at Calvary to consider their feelings toward, and misconceptions of, handicapped people. Our family and friends have visited Calvary and experienced the genuine love and friendliness there. They see how our church has been an excellent source of support for us. God is working in and through our small church. Our church strives to exemplify what Paul says in Romans 1:16-17:

"For I am not ashamed of the gospel, for it is the power of God for the salvation to everyone who believes, to the Jew first and also to the Greek. For in it the righteousness of God is revealed from faith for faith, as it is written, the righteous shall live by faith."

We have enjoyed serving at Calvary as the church has served us. Mark was on the Diaconate as chairman for three years and vice chairman for a year. We have taught Sunday school and Vacation Bible School. For a time we ran the sound system and handled the tape ministry, which was a blessing in itself. Our visits to the elderly and shut-ins were always just as big an encouragement to us as for them. Our daughter Katie plays viola for special music, we occasionally sing for offertory, and Richard, our next-to-oldest son, also helped Mark usher for a while. We do not just expect to receive from the church, even though they have so graciously and abundantly given to us, but we also want to give back to serve others and God. Bringing glory to God and sharing His love with others, especially our family at Calvary, is our ultimate goal for God alone deserves our highest praise and very lives.

Prayer:
Dear Lord, thank You for Your Word and for allowing us to come into Your presence and be able to go to church. Thank You for our church families and the blessing they are to us. Thank You for teaching us faith and trust in You.
In Jesus' name,
Amen

CHAPTER SIX

The Skies Parted and the Heavens Open

"Trust in the LORD with all your heart and lean not on your own understanding; in all your ways submit to him, and he will make your paths straight." – Proverbs 3:5-7

In the fall of 1986 we were still in denial that anything could possibly be seriously medically wrong with Cyndy even after she almost died at Thanksgiving. We didn't believe that Mark Jr. was perhaps "not normal" given his developmental and speech delays. Worried about Cyndy's health, Dr. Jay Piland went to the elders and asked for the church to help us pay to have our children tested for neurological disabilities. I had started to accept that maybe Mark Jr. was not doing all that other children his age was doing but Cyndy---no way would I agree that she was seriously handicapped. Mark Sr. and I and our families didn't want to believe that Cyndy could possibly die or be mentally handicapped. To me, Cyndy was just a normal child with febrile seizures that she would outgrow when she turned five or six at the latest. But severely handicapped? No, no way. Even so, deep down in my heart, I knew that something was not normal with Cyndy's mental development. I wanted to stick my head in the sand and not deal with the seriousness of her health issues.

The Lord had been working on me throughout the fall. He kept placing the thought on my heart that we needed to get better medical treatment for Cyndy and find out what was happening medically with Mark Jr.'s health; he had stopped talking immediately after Cyndy started to seizure. We figured that something was not right with Mark Jr., but we weren't sure what was really going on. One of the ladies at our church who worked with au-

Cyndy having fits over Cathy's doll.

tistic children recognized some of little Mark's behaviors but we didn't consider that he was autistic. Not Mark Jr. Not our children. I had been taught that you do not mention those types of things. They were secrets to keep quiet and keep within the family. Mental handicaps were something that family members were too embarrassed to speak out about. Family members were placed in a hospital somewhere and forgotten. I assumed that people were constantly pointing at me and laughing behind my back as if they were saying "poor girl, she just doesn't know what she has gotten herself in."

The second week of December 1986 I was out Christmas shopping for the family when Cyndy had an acute seizure. I called our children's physician, Dr. Forrest White, but he was not available that day. The practice told me that Dr. Bobby Garrison could see Cyndy instead. This was the beginning of our medical relationship with Dr. Garrison. He became our children's primary doctor. When he saw Cyndy after her seizure, he was very concerned that a neurologist was not following her more carefully since her seizures were so serious. I can still remember one time during that first year of Cyndy's seizures when she was hospitalized. Dr. Garrison was making rounds, and I was so stressed and not sure what was happening. Dr. Garrison came in, sat down, and told me what was happening. He stressed that Cyndy's seizures were serious and something could happen if they weren't treated appropriately. It had been over a year since Cyndy began having seizures. We agonized over constantly rushing her to the doctors or hospital. We felt helpless whenever she was sick. None of the doctors' methods seemed to help to improve her physical health condition.

Just before Christmas, with urging from the pastor and elders, Mark and I let the church make arrangements for us to see a neurosurgeon that Pastor Wardell knew in Philadelphia. I had gotten to where I was starting to break down. I wasn't handling Cyndy's seizures well. I was increasingly fearful that Cyndy would die. Money for the treatment was a significant barrier but the church then agreed to pay the bill for us to go and get medical treatment for Cyndy's seizures as well as Mark's testing for autism. Our appointment was set for January of 1987.

We set out on a Sunday morning in January 1987. Before we left, we said a quick prayer after hearing the weather report that indicated heavy snow all the way up the mid-Atlantic coast. We left home with both sets of parents urging us not to go because of the forecast. We left early in the morning hoping to miss the worst of the storm but by the time we reached the eastern shore of Virginia we ran into blizzard conditions. The snow obscured our visibility so much that we considered turning around and going home. Yet a small voice, incredible and amazing, spoke to our souls "keep going, don't turn back." The Holy Spirit was telling us to keep plowing forward to our destination reassuring us that things were going to turn out for the best. We needed to trust the Lord's leading.

We were determined to keep going, remembering that we were doing this for our little girl who needed essential medical attention. Our hopes for saving Cyndy's life hinged on this trip. We needed answers to our questions: why she was seizuring all the time? We kept praying and asking God what we should do, remembering that God had provided the means of transportation and the money for food and lodging as well as the medical expense. The Lord was supplying all the means for us to have Cyndy treated – that was the driving force keeping us moving onward, trusting God to get us there and back home safely without looking at the storm raging around us.

We could not believe our eyes, when we got to the Maryland/Delaware border. The snow lay piled up high on the side of the road, reminding us of Moses parting the Red Sea!

"Then Moses stretched out his hand over the sea, and the Lord caused the sea to go back by a strong east wind all that night, and made the sea dry land, and the waters were divided." - Exodus 14:21

The roads had been cleared and were dry all the way through Delaware. We were amazed at how the snow was plowed up. We have often wondered how the people and Moses felt when the Lord parted the Red Sea. We were in awe. We knew then, without a doubt, that God definitely wanted us to keep going and he was providing the direction. After that sign from the Lord nothing could prevent us from obtaining help for Cyndy. It was smooth sailing the rest of the trip to Philadelphia.

Our trip to Philadelphia.

The snow began falling in earnest after we arrived that night. We peered out the motel windows at the falling snow. We were given the most beautiful glimpse of Heaven seeing sparks of light glistening off the fluffy white snowfall. It reminded me of when I was a little girl and my grandfather would play in the snow with me. I could hear his laugh and see him pulling me on the sled and building a snowman. I had not seen this much snow since I was about nine or ten years old. Memories of snow cream and snowball fights came back and I began to miss my grandparents...

That night was very peaceful and quiet. No sound could be heard outside as the snow fell freely. The moonlight brightened the snow, making it seem as if sparkling glitter had been sprinkled. The snow reminded me how God makes us whiter than snow, even when Jesus' blood covers our sins. Seeing how the ground was covered I saw what God does with our sins when we come to Christ.

By Monday morning the southeastern region of Pennsylvania had two new feet of snow in addition to what was already on the ground when we arrived. Since we didn't have snow chains we couldn't drive around town but the children enjoyed playing in the snow outside our motel room. We enjoyed the huge snowdrifts, which are very rare in eastern Virginia. Mark Jr. and Cyndy had the biggest smiles on their faces; they both had seen snow but never so deep!

Cyndy and Mark Jr. were scheduled for three days of tests beginning on Monday but they were delayed a day by the snowstorm. The delay made us more anxious. What we would do if Cyndy had a seizure so far from her doctors? On Tuesday morning Cyndy and Mark Jr. both had tons of tests done to assess their brain function and development.

The doctors asked us countless questions. We wanted answers from the neurosurgeon, Dr. Spitz. Once testing was completed Dr. Spitz gave us some sobering news about Cyndy's medical condition. We could not have been prepared for what he told us. Cyndy, my baby girl would likely be profoundly handicapped. Her brain was underdeveloped and she would likely die in a few short years. I didn't want to hear this news from any doctor - not Dr. Spitz, not even the doctors back home that knew Cyndy well. I didn't want hear that something was terribly wrong with my daughter.

Dr. Spitz's voice seemed to echo while he told Mark and me that our daughter was mentally handicapped. While her brain was structurally there it was severely underdeveloped. Her brain's wiring and connectors would never fully develop to normal capacity. Over time the demands on Cyndy's brain and the frequency of her seizures would be so great that her brain would simply not be able to handle them anymore. We were devastated at the thought of our precious daughter not being able to do things that we take for granted. I refused to accept that Cyndy would not learn basic skills. I was determined to fight to give Cyndy the closest thing to a normal life as possible. I believed that she could get better. I WAS GOING TO PROVE THEM WRONG EVEN IF I HAD TO GO TO MY GRAVE PROVING THE FACT.

In addition to having to absorb the news about Cyndy we also learned that the testing indicated Mark Jr. was autistic with mental retardation. While the staff concluded that he was trainable, it was still a lot to take in. Our dreams for our family changed in a heartbeat.

Mark and I cried almost all the time we were in Pennsylvania. We worried about how we would tell our relatives that our little angel was gravely ill. The neurosurgeon could not tell us how much time we had left with her. He said she could go today or it could be 10 or 20 years from now. However he was clear that children like Cyndy - born with small brains - usually die before they reach the age of 20.

I was angry at God. My heart accused Him of being unjust and uncaring. How could a loving God be so cold-hearted and careless when He had seen to us getting to Pennsylvania safely? Even in my anger I knew that God forgave my hatred and rage toward Him because He did care dearly about me. He was not about to let my temper tantrum get in the way of His eternal unconditional love for me.

We made the best of the mini-vacation; we went to see the Liberty Bell, Independence Hall, and the Philadelphia Mint in between the children's medical tests. Our two good-natured children were much too young to remember the trip to Philadelphia or the snow, but Mark and I will never forget the trip, the memories we made, and what God showed us. Little Mark and Cyndy never complained about the tests or all the sightseeing. They went along with the ride and slept hard at night.

Once we returned home we started working with Dr. Bobby Garrison. He managed to get our insurance company to reimburse us our expenses for the test on the children. He worked with us to keep Cyndy going and to get the medical services we needed for Cyndy and Mark Jr. Other doctors in Dr. Garrison's office got involved with Cyndy's care including Dr. Kitty Meredith, Dr. George Koehl, Dr. Tony Thomas, Dr. Victor Mickunas, Dr. Carolyn Riegle, Dr. Murphy, and Dr. Forrest White. In addition, Dr. Garrison had gotten Dr. Chaves, the pediatric neurologist on board with Cyndy's case. Within the year we met Dr. Toor and, finally, Dr. Larry White. We were extremely blessed to find these doctors and to have their support. Some of these dear physicians and friends continue to be a part of our lives today.

This was the beginning of our long uphill battle but at least now we were moving in the right direction. We were getting Cyndy help for her seizures. They were getting under control. Although each step forward was small we were continually encouraged and amazed to see Cyndy do things that we were told she would never be able to do. God is good to us, and His faithfulness is everlasting. Our sorrow turned to joy when we returned home and found out I was pregnant with our third child Richard Wesley!

When we look back on that trip to Pennsylvania we can see how God was taming our hearts and molding us into His servants. God was chiseling away the hardness in our hearts and softening our spirits to His loving ways. Through the entire heartache that week we never were out of God's loving care. Even when we cried over Cyndy Christ was there shedding tears with us.

Prayer:
Thank you, Lord, for sustaining us through rough times in life. Your grace and mercy are sufficient even when things seem bleak. Thank you for the love you have shown us. Thanks for the sun that always shines after a rainy day.
In Christ,
Amen

CHAPTER SEVEN

He Giveth Power to The Faint

"Your words have supported those who stumbled; you have strengthened faltering knees." - Job 4:4

When we came back from Philadelphia our minds were cluttered with thoughts of how our family and lifestyle would be undergoing some radical changes over the weeks and years to come. The first thing on our agenda was to enroll Cyndy in a city-run infant program where specialists could work with her to stimulate her basic physical, mental, and cognitive development. The City of Chesapeake's Infant Stimulation Program incorporated speech and physical therapy designed to stimulate Cyndy's cognitive skills and get her more on track with what infants her age were doing. For example, while most normal babies develop gross motor skills on their own at 15 months Cyndy was learning to sit and stand with support of the specialists. The staff gave us the prognosis that Cyndy probably wouldn't walk by herself; if she ever walked it would be only very little and with assistance. Hearing those infant specialists talk about all the things Cyndy supposedly could not do angered me to no end. The more that professionals would tell me what Cyndy couldn't do, the more determined I became that my baby girl was going to prove them wrong with God's help.

At the age of one Cyndy was on various drugs including Pheno-

38

barbital. Phenobarbital was supposed to help control her febrile sei-zures but unfortunately it only made her lightheaded, unfocused, and very hyperactive! No matter how hard Cyndy tried, she could not sit briefly or remain in one place for very long even if she wanted to remain still. I can remember very well one of the doctor's appointments with Dr. Chaves. When he went to put Cyndy on his lap to examine her he couldn't hold her still long enough to completely check her over. The tighter he held her the more she would scream and squirm to get loose, making it VERY COMPLICATED for him to examine her thoroughly. She would butt her head against his chest and kick him – there was no settling her down – and my angel had become a devil-child!

The biggest problem with Phenobarbital was that it prevented Cyndy from making any real progress in sitting or walking without help; it really didn't help her seizures in any way. In order to provide Cyndy a chance to be able to walk, we asked Cyndy's doctors to take her off Phenobarbital and use a substitute. Dr. Chaves didn't hesitate with all the trouble she was giving him when it came to examining her! Once Cyndy's medication was changed things started happening. She mas-tered sitting and walking - Cyndy became our little miracle! Our faith in God was strengthened as we begin to see God's continuous mercy on Cyndy. Slowly she was mastering skills and her meds were gradually starting to help her seizures even if it was only for a short time.

Although we couldn't see God's tender mercy at first His grace was within Cyndy. As the psalmist says in Psalms the Lord's love and tender mercy and faithfulness toward us is unfailing.

> "Your steadfast love, O Lord, extends to the heavens,
> your faithfulness to the clouds.
> Your righteousness is like the mountains of God;
> your judgments are like the great deep;
> man and beast you save, O Lord." - Psalm 36:5-6

Each of the consultants from the Infant Stimulation Program worked diligently patterning Cyndy three days a week for an hour at a time, to help Cyndy learn and maintain new skills. The therapists taught me ways that I could assist in patterning Cyndy, helping strengthen her legs so that she would be able to sit and walk. We worked intensely to-gether as a team for Cyndy.

Cyndy's therapy didn't end when the in-home workers left – then it was my turn to begin working with her! I would use pillows as props to help her sit up, while encouraging her with rewards throughout the day to encourage her to sit by herself. Cyndy loved getting praise from us. We would hoot and holler, clap our hands and oh yes the cookies and the good ol' baby bottle filled with milk. Soon she was able to sit on her own and then we worked on pulling up to a standing position. We built upon each new skill to help her master the next skill.

I will never forget how excited I was the day that Cyndy surprised us by pulling herself up to a standing position in the playpen. We had just come home from a family vacation up to the mountains. I put Cyndy in her playpen while we got the remaining luggage out of the car. As we came back into the apartment Cyndy had pulled herself up into a standing position on her own greeted us! Cyndy gave me a look that said "now you owe me a cookie and a bottle of milk!" Yes she got her cookies and milk with bunches of hugs and kisses. Our hearts were filled with joy and laughter knowing that all the relentless work of trying to teach her to pull up to a standing position had paid off. We could see the fruits of our labors. Praise God! Thank you Jesus.

Seeing Cyndy standing for the first time on her own caused me to cry out in joy. PRAISE THE LORD one of our prayers had been answered! We had petitioned God with countless more prayers for God to help Cyndy learn more skills. We were praising the Lord for weeks for Cyndy's growth and development while watching and waiting for the next skill that Cyndy would master over the next few weeks, months, and years.

Our next big hurdle was to teach Cyndy to stand alone with no supports. This had been significantly difficult since her medications made her a little unsteady. By this time Cyndy was about 20 months old. I had been contemplating what we could do to encourage Cyndy to stand alone, when an excellent idea came to mind. Why not get a ten-gallon fish tank to see if the fish would intrigue her? The moment the thought crossed my mind I dashed down to the pet store and bought a hexagon ten-gallon fish tank and some large goldfish to put into the aquarium. I set the aquarium up and walked a way for a few minutes. When I returned I caught Cyndy standing at the tank looking at the big goldfish swimming around. She was so engrossed that she ended up taking her hands off the tank and stood alone for about 20 minutes before she realized that she was standing by herself without holding on to anything! However once she realized that she was standing alone, she would fall down. Over the next few days, Cyndy was completely mesmerized by the fish tank and would spend longer periods of time standing alone. She was confident and could hold her position without falling. We witnessed a true miracle! However the biggest challenge was ahead: walking.

Something fishy is going on.

Some days when we were working with Cyndy she would cry and protest but as her mother I was very determined not to let Cyndy give up. Oh yes, Cyndy loved being rewarded with praises and cookies even in times when she struggled to follow our commands. Cyndy was proud of herself when she accomplished something that was very stressful for her -- she would clap her hands together while shouting "yea" in delight. She honestly believed she had conquered THE WORLD! She and I were not quitters. There were times when something didn't go the way I thought it should have and I would throw my hands up in the air and be ready to give up; sometimes Cyndy was the same way. Other times I knew that I should continue to fight and Cyndy would do the same sometimes putting her mom to shame.

Learning to walk took lots of work and divine intervention. Cyndy was so stubborn at times that she would just plop down in the middle of the floor and refuse to get up and walk no matter what we did. I felt like we were grasping at straws when I got the idea to use a baby walker. It would help her move around the apartment more freely and, hopefully, become more secure in learning to walk. The physical therapist wasn't the happiest with me using a walker but Mark and I were willing to try anything to help Cyndy.

Finally I enticed her with a bottle; every time she came close to me I would move back a step or two to encourage her to take a step toward me. When she would get brave and take a step I would give her the bottle, clap, and cheer. Cyndy would smile big with tears streaming from her big blue pretty eyes. This method helped increase her self-confidence up and try to take more steps.

After two weeks of working nonstop egging her on in that type of fashion - teasing her with cookies and her bottle - Cyndy began walking by herself. Cyndy was 21 months old and once she realized that she could walk there was no stopping her from getting around! As thankful as we were that Cyndy had learned to walk, we were not sure if it was a blessing now that she could get around and be more mischievous.

She was swift on her feet but the older she got the less stable her legs were; she fell frequently and a couple of times we ended up in the ER because Cyndy needed stitches from her falling and splitting her head open on the floor or hitting the corner of a table. She gave us, her grandparents, and her doctors gray hairs with the way she would shake rattle and move to get to one place to another. She wasn't going to let anything stop her now!

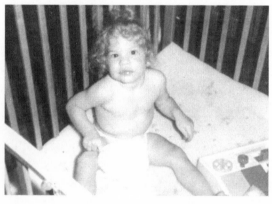

With Cyndy, clothes were often optional.

The doctors continued to tweak her medications to try and control her seizures. Dr. Chaves put her on one med that kept her from seizuring for about three months but then all of a sudden she would regress and he would have to add another drug. The seizures were shorter in duration and we were able to control them at home instead of having to take her to the hospital all the time. Mark and I had begun to feel at ease that the seizures were no longer life-threatening. However we knew it was only a matter time before the seizures would get out of control again.

Talking proved to be too difficult a hurdle for Cyndy to master, yet she tried her best. We prayed and prayed; we pleaded with the Lord to loosen her tongue. However God did not choose to allow Cyndy to communicate verbally here on earth. She did learn a few small words, such as "eye," "nose," "ear," and "mouth," and at the end of her life, she had begun to say "hair." She loved to name the parts of her face to anyone who would listen. Even though she couldn't have much verbal dialogue with another person, she managed to get her needs across to us.

She learned how to wave a goodbye, although she copied what she saw which was our hand turned toward her so she would turn her hand toward herself to wave bye-bye. Cyndy would lead you to the sink for water or grab your hands to play her favorite game - patty cake. You could tell that she knew the exact order of the motions because if you tried to leave some of the motions or words out she wouldn't let you. What really amazed people about Cyndy was that when she wanted to play patty-cake or

Toys, toys everywhere, on Christmas day.

name the parts of her face she would demand eye contact!

Cyndy had a stubborn nature and always surprised us with what she could accomplish by working so hard and wanting it so badly. God blessed her with a very determined spirit and a strong will to live. Nothing could hold her down for very long. Even when she was incredibly sick she would rest for a time and then be up and eager to be on the go again!

Cyndy's strength and courage was a living testimony of how the Lord uses a handicapped child to do His will. I often wondered about how, in her own way, she must have communed with God. He must have shown Himself to her that she trusted Him so much in the middle of her trials. We believe that God had generously provided the physical and emotional courage to this two-year-old child. His grace was so rich and free for her.

"I can do all things through Christ who strengthens me." - Phil.4:13

Even though Cyndy was significantly language delayed, we often noticed her mimicking sounds to favorite old hymns during church. She would smile, clap, and coo loudly when we walked to the front entrance of church each Sunday morning. Mark and I would have loved to have known what was going through Cyndy's head. What made her tick? Why did she insist on so meticulously doing things her way? How did she have such a content spirit? Her relationship with God must have been on such a deep level that Mark and I could not comprehend it here on earth. We will have to wait until we arrive in Heaven to understand their relationship.

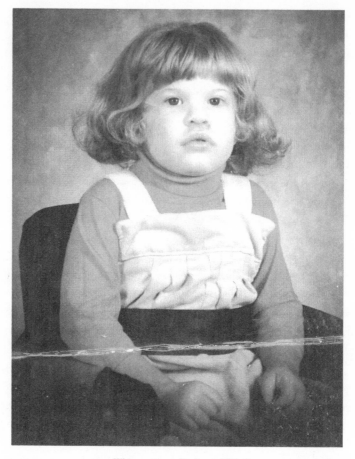

Where are you, Dr. Larry White?

Many times we thought of just how much Cyndy had visualized or how much God must have appeared to her that Cyndy wasn't afraid when she had her medical crises. Could Cyndy have been aware of heavenly matters that were impossible for us to see or understand? Some of her actions and gestures led us to believe that she must have seen something (probably angels). Yet is it possible too that she had actually seen Christ? When she was weary and felt she had no strength left God must have given her the emotional strength to keep going so that people around her could see Jesus in her life. Christ gives strength to the weary as He must have done just that for Cyndy!

"He gives power to the faint,
and to him who has no might he increases strength.

44

Even youths shall faint and be weary,
and young men shall fall exhausted;
but they who wait for the Lord shall renew their strength;
they shall mount up with wings like eagles;
they shall run and not be weary;
they shall walk and not faint." - Isaiah 40:29-31

Cyndy had such a strong spirit that when she was sick she would only be down long enough for a nap and then be on the go once again. While in the hospital, Cyndy would be hydrated through an IV and meds to stop her seizures. Then she would be climbing out of the crib and making her way to the elevator.

Dr. Chaves stepped aside when Dr. Larry White was doing a study on a new medication. When she was in the hospital, she would cry until Dr. White would come, take her out of the crib, and carry her on rounds with him. One time when I was kidding Dr. White about Cyndy sweet-talking him into taking her out of the crib, he told me that he couldn't look at Cyndy directly in the eyes when she was in her crib because she would melt him with her "poor me" eyes. He would then take her out of the crib and let her make rounds with him until she was tired, or he was finished making his rounds and was ready to leave the hospital.

Prayer:
Thank you, Lord, for giving us the determination to live and to be able to get up and go each day. Thank you for the ability to walk, and being able to talk, and worship you.
In Christ,
Amen

CHAPTER EIGHT

Entertaining Angels Unaware

"Be not forgetful to entertain strangers: for thereby some have entertained angels unawares." - Hebrews 13:2

Our family was growing and Cyndy's medical needs were changing. Our second son Richard was born on August 6, 1987. Two days short of a year later Mark and I met Dr. Larry E. White when Cyndy was readmitted to CHKD by Dr. Garrison for non-stop seizures. At first I tried to talk Dr. Garrison out of putting Cyndy in the hospital; I wasn't overly worried about the seizures. Dr. Garrison was and his orders were "GO RIGHT NOW TO THE HOSPITAL, NO GOING HOME FIRST PERIOD."

Dr. White happened to be the neurologist on duty for the neurology group during that week. When Dr. Garrison had put Cyndy in the hospital he told me that he thought I would like this doctor. Dr. White was new to the group and Dr. Garrison wanted me to try him since I had been very critical of some of the doctors. Cyndy's seizure medications were no longer working and the doctors needed to make some changes.

The first thing I remember about Dr. White when he came into the room to introduce himself was that he was such a young doctor. He surprised me by pulling up a chair and sitting down. He shared the strategy he had to bring her seizures back under control over the next two to three days before sending her back home. He explained his planned course of action in detail and wanted to know if we had any questions. He was in no hurry to leave.

After that first meeting it seemed like Dr. White was always the physician on call when Cyndy had her worst bouts of seizures. We thanked God when he was on duty when Cyndy would seizure; we knew that he would do everything to the best of his ability to control those seizures. It happened so frequently that we began to think Cyndy knew when to have her seizures to catch Dr. White and not the other doctors!

DR. WHITE: Cyndy and I first met at the Children's Hospital of the King's Daughters (CHKD) in Norfolk, Virginia during one of her many bouts with seizures that needed observation and often medication adjustments. I had just gotten out of the Air Force and returned to the Tidewater area which over time I began to consider home during my stay as a general pediatrician. I was trying to get used to my role in Cyndy's case as a consulting physician. Consulting physicians answer questions and give advice, while attending physicians provide the preventative medical care to the patient. I wanted to make sure that even though I may only see her one time, I gave the best recommendations possible. Her pediatricians were a fantastic group of caring and capable doctors who treated her for years and knew her well.

As I began reviewing Cyndy's story, it was clear that adversity should have been her middle name. Her mom's pregnancy was anything but ideal, with her twin dying after only two months and the rest of the pregnancy marked by bleeding, attempted miscarriage, anxiety, and uncertainty. Cyndy's birth was not the smoothest transition into the real world either, with her aspirating amniotic fluid into her lungs and needing breathing support for a while. However after a brief course of antibiotics she was ready to go home as if everything was perfect; this rapid turnaround and rebound from whatever adversity came along would be repeated throughout her entire life.

Her first few months of life were uneventful, but after her first few well-baby exams, there was concern that her head and brain weren't growing as well as they should be. Before her first birthday she had several episodes of convulsions associated with fever. Even though these seizures were with a high fever her doctors were wondering if she had an underlying brain problem and that these weren't just "febrile" seizures. Both Phenobarbital and Dilantin were not controlling them and Tegretol was added without much benefit. EEG studies had not shown a persistent abnormality.

By the time she was 15 months old Cyndy was on three seizure medications that weren't working very well. Her parents took her to the Spitz Institute in Pennsylvania where EEG studies confirmed a diffuse generalized seizure focus, and scans showed an underdeveloped brain. Metabolic tests on blood and urine didn't isolate any particular cause. However, the information did tremendously help direct our medications and we began a new combination including both Depakene and Mysoline--medications that are certainly potent but also quite risky to children of her age. Her seizures stabilized for months, but then over time it became obvious she needed a new medication--but what?

Fortunately for Cyndy our institution was one of a few studying a new drug called Mogadon; it was in the same class of medications as Valium and Ativan but designed for day-to-day control of seizures rather than emergency treatment. It was being tested on children only with certain seizure types and there were significant restrictions. However Cyndy qualified and her parents jumped at the opportunity to try something new. This is where I came in, first treating her in the children's hospital and then looking after Cyndy after Dr. Enrique Chaves, her neurologist since her infancy, left the region. Getting her on Mogadon was the best thing we ever did; for a long time it was - and had to be - her "Miracle Drug."

I treated Cyndy in the hospital a bunch of times for prolonged seizures, and every time I was worried that she would lose some brain function. Since she already had significant physical challenges, no language ability, and unsteady balance I came up with some songs that would react to in a special way. One was the old song "B-I-N-G-O" but I changed the song to sing "C-Y-N-D-Y and Cyndy was her name-o!" She loved that one. I would sometimes chant to her "cyn-DEE, cyn-DEE, Cyndee with a Y!" and she would throw her arms up and out to form a "Y." If she had recovered from a seizure quickly and gave me a forlorn look I would cap off her IV line and take her on rounds with me at the hospital. The hospital was smaller then, and the wagons we use now with children weren't available then, so I would just carry her. She liked it and she really wasn't that heavy. When I would chant "cyn-DEE with a Y!" she would act like she was trying to get the nurses and med students to do the wave and often succeeded!

Despite what other people told me, Cyndy never spoke a word to me – in the hospital the nurses often said she didn't have to. But there was one time I was writing "Cindy" absent-mindedly in her chart and heard, "Dr. White it's with a "y." There was no one else there, and she was giving me that look.

Once Mark and I had gotten to know Dr. White we wanted him to take over as Cyndy's primary neurologist. When we asked him to take over Cyndy's care he was very gracious but didn't want to step on his partners' toes. He told us to call him with any questions or concerns we had about Cyndy.

About a year after seeing Dr. White in the hospital I began seeing him around Central Elementary School (a school at the time for handicapped children) doing physicals. He encouraged me to get actively involved with parents of children with seizure disorders and to read up and understand as much as possible on epilepsy. As I read more about seizures I realized that parents needed a place to go and get quality assistance. After prayer and careful thought I approached Dr. White about helping me start a support group for parents in the Tidewater area. He was very supportive. He has taught me to aim high and do my very best.

When Cyndy's care was finally transferred to Dr. White he was researching the drug Mogadon. Cyndy's back-to-back seizures had returned and we were going to the hospital frequently. When Cyndy wasn't getting better we were willing to help the drug research by letting them try it on Cyndy.

Cyndy loved Dr. White dearly because he had such a caring personal interest in her and our entire family, much like a father figure. I have seen very few doctors that clearly exhibit the degree of significant care that Dr. White had for Cyndy and all his patients he has in his care. Most doctors tend to be very clinical and detached from their patients, almost for their own emotional protection. However, Dr. White was unique; he allowed himself to be vulnerable with our family. He was not afraid to show his emotions or be truly involved in our lives. He is a very meek person with a big heart.

DR. WHITE: I have been a doctor for almost 35 years, and almost all of that time has been devoted to treating children. I've spent 20 years treating children with neuralgic conditions and during that period I would have to say that I've seen almost every conceivable type of reaction to, adjustment to, recovery from, and progression of neuralgic injuries and illness.

When people think about sickness and injury, they think in terms of getting well and how long it's going to take them (or their friend or loved one) to recover. As a physician, it's my calling and my duty to help them do that. There are times that I do a great deal for them and with them, and there are also times I can do very little, at least medically speaking. This can be very difficult on the parents and siblings, not to mention the patient, and everyone has different ways of dealing with the sheer stress. A very important thing to remember is that people with injury to the nervous system often have to deal with quality of life issues, as well as living or dying. As care providers and caregivers, we may have a very different idea of what matters most to the patient, and vice-versa. Add to that the communication gap that exists between ages, genders and cultures, and I hope that people can appreciate the size and number of "potholes" that exist in a person's road to recovery, as well as just surviving daily life.

Doctors, being people, have a wide range of interests and styles, and I wish sometimes that we could all be like the stereotypes on television – characters that can solve complicated illness in an hour, make house calls anywhere in a large city, and still have time for an office practice, almost kill a patient in 56 minutes as long as they get the answer in 57, or have expertise in multiple specialties including surgery and pathology (while working for the FBI)! The role of doctors in the health care system is changing as more science and technology fill the hours of our day. And the unrealistic expectations to frequently see more people in less time become an insurer-driven reality. We are fighting a "case" driven wave that threatens to dehumanize the most human of qualities-- taking care of one another in body and spirit.

Getting ready for the harvest party.

As a doctor, my particular style has been to acknowledge the bad things that happen and may continue to happen, but also emphasize the positive and work as best I can for a better tomorrow. We all know that the deeper the "hole" of illness is, the harder it is to climb out. I push my patients to climb as hard as they can while avoiding things that would enlarge the hole. And while that sounds simple and straightforward we all know that the reality is vastly different. Doctors that have practiced for a while have all seen people get better from illness, fight hard and long but succumb, cope with tragedy, deal with adversity, grieve, hope, pray, and resolve. I am sure that other docs like me, even though we've treated thousands of people, have those patients and families that are "special." By that I don't infer that they are any better than anyone else or necessarily that their problem was rarer or more serious, but that the relationship between us was such that the mere mention of their name elicits a flood of memories and emotional ups and downs so thick that, like a fog or a snowstorm, you try to wipe it away from your face. I have certainly treated "special" children. Like Cyndy.

There are times I wonder where her name came from. I see moms giving their children all manner of names and variations on conventional names, just spelling it differently to make it "unique." But Cyndy didn't need an extra letter to be special; she did that all by herself.

Seizures are, other than someone choking, the scariest nontraumatic event you can witness at any age. But in a child I think there is an even more emotional reaction. While Cyndy's convulsive seizures were the life-threatening ones, she had other more subtle types of seizures as well and they involved jerking once, flopping on the floor or staring ahead. Her EEG patterns and some other aspects of her seizures made it unclear whether she represented one of the several "severe seizure syndromes" as we

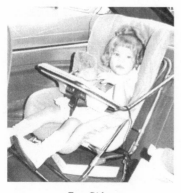

Easy Rider.

described them at the time. With Cyndy's lack of coordination and no language ability sometimes determining how she fell (if it was an accident or on account of seizure) was tough. I didn't want to change her meds around willy-nilly so we had to keep careful watch over when and how she fell. If she wobbled, slid, or simply went "kaboom" on her tush that was balance related. When she jumped or dropped like a stone that was considered a seizure.

Every neurologist who treats seizures, especially the kind that Cyndy had wishes that they could find that special "lightning in a bottle" medication. Mogadon wasn't that, but it was close. Within weeks of starting on Mogadon Cyndy had a major problem with her platelet count and her hemoglobin levels dropped rather abruptly forcing us to hospitalize her again. Fortunately, it was one of those times where, like cancer patients, her blood tests looked awful but she looked good. After we stopped both her Tegretol and Depakene her levels came back up. With the Mogadon we had the luxury of stopping medications rather than trying to guess which one it was, how much to back off and when, or worry about things getting really bad while we are deciding. Just as she did as a baby, Cyndy had a way of shrugging off catastrophe and going on with her life—the next year and change were arguably the best times of her life.

Little Beauty

For the next year we watched Cyndy grow and develop a bit. Further investigations into why her brain didn't develop properly disclosed no evidence of a degenerative disorder, a genetic syndrome, or other problem. The genetic aspect became very important as her two brothers got older and showed a slowly growing head and autistic spectrum disorder but without the seizures. All three children developed multiple behavior problems that required medication for control. Since Cyndy was on an investigational medication we were getting blood tests so often that she got used to them which was a relief. After a year or so very subtle seizures caused us to increase her Mogadon levels. Once we reached the maximum dosage for the study design we had to try others. Cyndy still tended to have rather scary seizures with high fevers and on occasion when her fevers reached 105-106°F there was concern that the fevers themselves may be doing some harm.

Close to her fifth birthday Cyndy had another close call that no one could have predicted. There was a brief shortage of Mogadon due to a manufacturing problem and even though we tapered the dose slightly prior to running out and used every other "cousin" drug that we had, including Valium and Ativan, she was scaring the nurses with her seizure clusters. Despite it all Cyndy never needed the ICU other than for attentive monitoring. After things settled down she would give you a look that assured you that whatever came along she would beat it. She would get up out of her bed, toddling along next to me with all the grace of Bambi on ice.

Dr. White cared vigilantly for Cyndy. I know she wasn't his easiest patient, and in fact was probably was one of his hardest cases in some ways. However if I know Cyndy, she has been looking down and smiling at him, thankful for all the care he gave her over the years. She might even be blowing kisses to him and Dr. Garrison, knowing that had it not been for their excellent care she might not have lived as long as she did here on earth.

Prayer:
Lord,
We thank you for such wonderful doctors that you had sent our way. We are thankful for doctors such as Drs. White and Garrison and for their wonderful care they have given Cyndy and the rest of our children. Thank you for giving them the medical knowledge and setting them apart for your precious children. Lord we thank you for all the Christian doctors that confess You as Lord and Savior.
In Jesus Name,
Amen

CHAPTER NINE

God's Special Child From Above

"Whoever humbles himself like this child is the greatest in the kingdom of heaven." - Matthew 18:4

Cyndy had been a very pleasant, happy-go-lucky child despite being plagued with numerous health problems. For the most part she was no different from any other child her age; she had the same emotions and wants. But Cyndy had ways of showing the unconditional love of Christ to everyone she met. She was highly inquisitive, obstinate, playful, and courageous with unlimited affection to share with those around her. Like any other child she knew how to push boundaries to get whatever she wanted. In some ways it was like she was a cuddly infant stuck in a teenage body – like she just did not want to grow up.

She had the IQ of a toddler and yearned for the security of baby items. At times, I wondered if she may have liked the items for how they felt and smelled. She was fascinated by the kanga-rock-a-roo infant seats. She was constantly strapping herself in them and would rock to her heart's content. Because Cyndy was so highly attracted to newborn items she would often kick her younger brothers and sister out of their stroller seats or grab their baby bottles or blankets for herself. Her younger siblings were not always thrilled about her antics, but Cyndy never intended to be ugly to them. She was just a delightful baby at heart herself. She was not too thrilled about sleeping in a big girl's bed and became angry with her baby brother because he was using the crib instead. We honestly thought that she would rather have a bed since she could more easily climb out of it, yet for some reason Cyndy just preferred sleeping in cribs. The only time that

And not one driving lesson...

she did not like the crib was when she was in the hospital because she would have to work hard to get the bubble top off in order to escape!

Cyndy always demanded complete eye contact from anyone she met. When Cyndy wanted to play patty-cake or name the parts of her face, she would coo loudly while gesturing for someone to sit down so she could climb on their lap. If for some reason you didn't give her the eye contact she had expected she would turn your face around to make complete eye contact. What made it so remarkable is that children with severe disabilities like Cyndy rarely are able to, or want to, make complete eye contact or interact with other people.

If Cyndy had a seizure we knew she was going to be fine afterward when she would take our hands and want to play patty cake. Cyndy would not even try to play patty cake with us until she knew that she was going to be all right. Then Lord help us! She would grip our hands with a vise-like grip, adamant about wanting us to play with her. After she tired of playing patty-cake she would jump to naming the parts of her face, letting everyone know that she was ready to get up and go now that the seizure was over.

Cyndy was very adventurous. She would get into everything that she could touch. She was curious about everything I brought home, especially boxes. When Cyndy saw me with a box her eyes would get big and the wheels in her brain would start turning. She loved boxes more than the toys inside them at times. She would take the toys out and throw them to the side so that she could climb inside. The amazing thing was that she didn't care what size the box was - she would try to climb in whether she would fit or not. The bigger the box the happier she was. When I put

Cyndy's toys back in her toy box she would come behind me and empty the toys back out and play inside the box for hours. Cleaning up the toys was useless before she went to bed. Once she fell fast asleep inside her large toy box. I put pillows and blankets in to make it comfortable and left her there peacefully for her afternoon nap.

Cyndy loved food and was always the first one to the table. If she got there before you she might even try to swipe your food if you weren't fast enough! You had to watch your plate because she would help herself! Cyndy knew very well how to feed herself but there were times that she felt lazy and wanted someone else to wait on her. She would grab my hand and coo at me and then forcefully guided my hand with a fork full of food to her mouth. She loved to play "airplane" with her food and laugh the whole time. Her favorite food was macaroni and cheese and baked potatoes. If she didn't like food on her plate she would sneak it to the cat under the table. No matter what game you tried to play to get her to eat something if she didn't like it she would just turn away and make a raspberry sound!

Cyndy had an engineer's mind – she liked to take things apart to see how they were put together. One Christmas Cyndy decided to take all the decorations off the tree, I presume to see how the Christmas tree was put together. Thank God back then we had a live Christmas tree because she would have taken the tree apart too! I knew she was up to mischief when I heard only silence. I glanced from around the corner of the kitchen to see her quietly grabbing the assorted Christmas ornaments off the tree and piling them into a chair. Cyndy was so adorable. She was trying ever so hard not to make any noise. She took each ball and turned it all sorts of ways to see its beauty before laying it down in the chair. I believe she would have pulled down the entire tree if I had not caught and stopped her! Cyndy loved the miniature lights that illuminated every inch of the tree. They mesmerized her. She was awestruck by the brightness of colors. If Cyndy weren't undressing the tree she was checking out the gifts under the tree. If she shook the box and it made a noise she would unwrap it before we even knew what was happening!

When Cyndy was bored downstairs she would head for her room. She couldn't stand for her clothes to be neatly placed in the dresser drawers. She would empty out her dresser drawers and then climb in. No matter how many times I would come along behind and tidily put the clothes back in the drawer; she would take them back out and climb back in!

With Cyndy around, there was never a dull moment. When she was in her wooden playpen but wanted to be at the other side of the room she would stick her foot out and push until she got to her destination. She was the only one of our six children that figured out how to move the playpen across the room to get wherever she wanted to go. Obviously she was going to find her way or get whatever her little heart desired!

If I heard Cyndy clapping her hands, talking very loudly, while knocking against the window I knew I better run upstairs quickly to see what mischief she had gotten herself into. Many times I would find her stark naked standing in front of her window! Cyndy had no modesty and did not care that she was nude - she was proud of what she had and wanted the world to see it too!

When Cyndy graduated from the infant program she went into the handicapped preschool program. She was a typical child, pushing the boundaries as far as possible and keeping her teachers busy. Once the teacher placed a rug at the door of the classroom as a boundary to let Cyndy know how far she could go without getting in trouble. Well, Cyndy figured a way to get around the boundary by pushing her chair close to the door, then inching little by little until she had the rug outside the room, making her getaway.

Cyndy also had a special chair at school designed to help calm her when she was overly hyperactive. However when she was still strapped in the chair she would simply rock herself back and forth until she was able to get up and walk around with the chair on her back; a sight to see!

The last year of preschool she was chosen to play Rudolph the Red-Nosed Reindeer in her class Christmas play. Cyndy's teacher sat on the floor next to Cyndy and gave her a bell to ring. Suddenly Cyndy threw the bell across the stage and took the costume antlers off, escaped her seat, and ran across the stage. She was a strong-willed child, but you could not help but to love her. She just had so much life and excitement, not even her illness could take that away from her.

Cyndy would blow kisses and exhibit the prettiest, sweetest smile for the bus drivers and aides that helped her get on and off the bus lift at school. They loved her back and were very protective of her. The only thing that the bus drivers didn't like was that Cyndy had a way of getting out of her seat belts, no matter what restraint they used! The transportation department would come up with a new idea on how to keep her in her seat and it would work for a few days. But then she would cleverly learn how to get out of the new restraint. She earned the snappy nickname "Houdini" from her bus drivers because of her "escape artist" ways.

Cyndy found comfort in simple things like her little red wagon. When Cyndy was not feeling well or had a seizure she would climb into her wagon. It doubled as her bed during the day and it was a superb way of calming her down when she was extremely hyperactive. At naptime she would grab a pillow and cushion from the sofa, crawl in her wagon, and take her nap. If she wanted someone to take her for a ride she would climb into her wagon, sit and pout until someone came along and pulled her around the yard or even neighborhood. If we got tired she would make sad puppy dog eyes. If that didn't work she would start cooing loudly or crying, causing me to come out and see what was wrong. Her brothers and sister learned very quickly that if Cyndy cried Mom would come out and fuss at them for picking on her; they knew to keep pulling her even if they were tired! Cyndy knew how to manipulate her siblings to do anything she wanted them to do. She had that down.

She loved going to Grand Bobbie and Gaga's house because she knew they and my brother Jimmy would pull her around their yard and the neighbor's yard until the cows came home. She would become extremely excited when we would get close to my parent's house; all we had to do was get on Route 460 and she would start cooing loudly and clapping her hands.

As much as Cyndy liked getting into things, she also liked getting out of them! Cyndy nearly threw my parents, brother Jimmy and his wife Toni, younger sister Cathy and her husband Patrick into a panic when they could not find her one day while they were keeping all the kids to give Mark and me a weekend to ourselves. Everyone looked all over the house and up and down the street looking for Cyndy. Finally my parent's neighbor found her happily playing on their porch swing. She gave them a look like she wasn't lost - she merely wanted to play on Pearl's porch, as if to say, "I'm just swinging, what's your problem?"

Cyndy put me into sheer panic one afternoon coming home from a doctor's appointment. I had taken Joel out of the car first and brought him into the house. When I returned to get Cyndy, she had already gotten out and was nowhere in sight. Where could she have gone in such a short time? I was so scared I could barely tell our neighbors Steve and Kathy that Cyndy was missing. When I was finally able to speak the neighbors quickly went off in different directions looking for her. When

I went back to the house to call the police I spotted her sitting peacefully on the couch. Apparently Cyndy thought she was helping me by getting out of the car, coming into the house, and sitting on the couch. Finding her I dropped to my knees, thanking the Lord for letting us find her safe and secure and that no harm had been brought to her.

I'm the baby, not Richard. Yay!

Even the hospital staff could barely keep up with Cyndy. One time she actually made it out of a secured crib – with a bubble top bolted on - and got into the elevator before the nurses even noticed she was gone! When we got the call from the nurses that Cyndy had slipped out of the crib and been found on the elevator by Dr. White, Mark and I thought they were kidding. Given her mental handicaps no one could have imagined she would have known how to wriggle the top off the crib and climb out, sneak past the nurses, and get on an elevator. Cyndy even knew how to sweet talk Dr. White into taking her out of the crib. She would hoodwink him into pulling her around in the wagon while he made rounds. Cyndy knew all she had to do was blow him kisses and he would melt.

Dr. White's notes to his colleague Dr. Garrison, Dr. White wrote "...she would be as wild as ever. She is in her 'raging bull' mode today, thundering around the office, knocking over nearly everything in her path." Another time he wrote "she is mute, impulsive, and once again attacks the office in a lurching 'bull in a china shop' type of gait." Everybody had to clear the way when she wanted something because she was going to get what she wanted no matter what she had to do to get it!

As if keeping the doctors, teachers, and us running wasn't enough she would keep the deacons at our church on their toes too! Deacons, including our friend Bill Tuck, would take Cyndy for walks during the service to try to settle her down. When Bill had deacon chores to do during the service he would take Cyndy with him and let her run up and down the hallways of the church. Even when Bill was done Cyndy would keep him busy playing patty cake, climbing on him, and wanting him to carry her around wherever he went. She brought a completely new meaning to the deacon's role of servant!

Cyndy could also be very mature and focused given her true mental age. She participated in the Special Olympics every May from the time she was two years old and won countless first place ribbons for the 10-meter run. She would laugh while she ran - it was truly a beautiful sight to watch.

We all have cherished possessions and Cyndy's was a yellow stuffed teddy bear that played "Jesus Loves Me" which Mark and I gave to her on her first Christmas. She and that bear were inseparable. She slept with it and carried it to school and took it with her on numerous hospital stays. She used the bear to soothe the uncertainties. She almost always carried that bear by the ear with her pincher grasp. If Cyndy was sick or in need of an injection the nurses had to give one to Cyndy and an imaginary one to the yellow bear. If Cyndy got an ice cream, or was given fluids to drink when she was sick, the nurses also would put a straw to the bear's mouth to encourage Cyndy to drink. Cyndy would bring the bear to us countless times during the day so that we would wind it up. She always wanted it wound before taking a nap or going to sleep for the night.

No wonder Christ said in the gospels that He wanted the children to come sit in His lap. Christ loved children. In the gospels of Matthew, Mark, and Luke, Christ told the people to bring the children to Him and that we need to be just like them in order to inherit the Kingdom of God.

> *"Then children were brought to him that he might lay his hands on them and pray. The disciples rebuked the people, but Jesus said, 'Let the little children come to me and do not hinder them, for to such belongs the kingdom of heaven.' And he laid his hands on them and went away."* - Matthew 19:13-15

Prayer:
Thank you, Lord, for all the funny things we remember about our children and the memories that You give us to remember them. When we feel down we can rejoice thinking about our children and how they would keep us going. Thank you for showing us their love and Your love through these memories. May we be like children and come to You.

In Christ's name,
Amen

CHAPTER TEN

And the Lame Walk
and the Blind See

"If you can! All things are possible for one who believes."
- Mark 9:23

Mark and I believe that children – all children, regardless of their physical and mental health – are blessings from the Lord. We were happy to continue being blessed with more children. Our second daughter, Katie, was born on April 25, 1990 and our third son, Buddy, was born right on her heels on March 6, 1991.

As our family was expanding Cyndy was growing and her health problems continued.

DR. WHITE: The following years were touch and go at times. Her pediatrician, Dr. Bobby Garrison, was very clever to treat Cyndy with preventative antibiotics during the winter, a tactic that certainly is not recommended for everyone. With Mogadon as her mainstay, we added other medications when she had increased seizures not triggered by illness. We added Tegretol back at one point, new medications Felbatol and Lamictal, and some old ones including the dreaded Valproate which at her age we knew she could tolerate. Cyndy gave us a scare just after her sixth birthday when she was found in her bed blue one morning. Pertinent questions came fast: Did she have a seizure and aspirate and partially obstruct her airway? Did she have a "near miss" SUDS episode, which is a sad phenomenon occurring in epileptic patients when they die unexpectedly in their sleep presumably from a seizure? Did she have a spasm of her airway as part of a seizure? Did someone in the house try to smother her? Cyndy looked unconcerned as usual. When she spiked a fever the next day to 105°F without evidence of aspiration we wondered if all the events were related to an illness.

In January 1992, I got a call at about 9:30 one school morning that Cyndy had spiked a fever and was having back-to-back seizures. Thank God for miracles - Dr. White was once again on call at the hospital. Because of our insurance, we had to first go through the primary doctor before we could see the specialist or go to the emergency room.

By then she was having exceptionally long seizures, "status epilepticus," with all the breathing problems associated with it. Cooling her off became a priority, and as cold as it was that day, the paramedics opened all the windows and turned the air conditioner on full blast.

Our Pastor - Mark Bender - lived a couple miles from Dr. Garrison's office. After seeing Cyndy code, I could not stand to go with her in the ambulance fearing that she would die. I honestly thought if I didn't go to the hospital, Cyndy would not die. Thank God big Mark was with me and went with Cyndy to the hospital in the ambulance. I went to the Bender's; Pastor Mark helped round up our two children at school along with the other two children being watched by his wife Marlene. I had done everything possible to keep from going; Pastor Mark had to literally drag me there.

As Pastor Mark and I walked down the hall to the emergency room patient holding area we were talking. Cyndy heard my voice and responded. For five hours, Dr. White and Mark could not get her to respond but my voice woke her out of a coma-like state.

DR. WHITE: From that point on every time something unusual occurred medically with Cyndy she was treated for infection first.

When she was healthy Cyndy actually had time to enjoy

school, church, and other normal childhood activities. I don't think she was bothered about not talking or walking well; she would always get up after seizures, falls, and accidents. Despite her problems Cyndy was enthusiastic about just "being here."

Her attitude was uplifting and inspiring to watch.

As Cyndy grew taller and heavier walking became more difficult. Her legs muscles were getting weaker and it was getting harder for her to walk without falling. She was in constant danger of getting hurt from running into walls or hitting corners of end tables.

DR. WHITE: I remember my girl having falls that could rival what I've seen on the ski slopes or at skateboard parks. And this was with scrutiny at home and in the hospital that was at least as tight as it would be today. Despite the falls, she never fell down the stairs, broke a bone, or injured her head. But she did have some events worthy of YouTube! She was consistent about just getting up and going on with things – it just seemed that she accepted the falls as part of the ambulation. It didn't deter her from pushing her limits. If your parents or doctor saying "Oh God! Cyndy!" counts as a prayer there were many, many prayers said on Cyndy's behalf!

When Cyndy was eight she hit a growth spurt which caused her legs to weaken tremendously. Doctors Garrison and White became extremely concerned about Cyndy's feet turning in. None of us wanted her to stop walking.

In the summer of 1994 our doctors had us meet Dr. Sheldon St. Clair, an orthopedic specialist. We heard that he was one of the most tender and caring doctors at CHKD. Other parents we knew from school told us about some of the things he done to assist their children who were worse off than Cyndy. When we met him, we saw what others had said about him were true. He was moved to tears when he saw how deformed Cyndy's legs were, yet how badly she wanted to keep walking. We could tell that he felt it was his duty and power to give every child a chance to walk or to be able to keep walking.

Dr. St. Clair did various tests to determine the extent of her leg problems and to decide on the best way to correct them over time. He told us that there would be three surgeries over three years, each one spaced a year apart, to strengthen and straighten out her legs. We asked Dr. St. Clair if he would schedule the operation later in the fall. I was pregnant with our sixth (and last!) child, Joel, who ended up being born by c-section 10 weeks early on September 30, 1994.

In November we were ready for Cyndy's surgery which would be the first of three complicated operations. The doctor did bilateral anterior and posterior tibia tendon split transfers which would gradually improve her walk. Cyndy had to be put into traction after the surgery. The very first night Cyndy was sleeping a lot and the nurses believed it was safe for Mark and me to eat dinner next door at Norfolk General. While we were out Dr. Garrison stopped by the room to check on Cyndy. Even though she was still sluggish from the drugs given for pain, she woke up when she heard Dr. Garrison's voice. Cyndy decided that she had enough of the hospital and that it was time for her to get up and go about her merry way. With Dr. Garrison in the room Cyndy assumed it was play time and she wanted to give him hugs and kisses - nothing was going to hold her down any longer. Every nurse in the unit raced to get Cyndy to lie back down and not pull off the weights that were holding her legs in traction. She gave them one big scare, and made the nurses earn their pay that night!

We were paged over the loudspeaker to come back to the room stat. Dr. Garrison had spotted us at Norfolk General and pleaded with us to go back to CHKD to relieve the nurses that were trying to keep Cyndy in her bed. There was no chance of leaving the ward to get anything to eat or drink or even getting a breather during that hospital stay. When the next meal came around the nurses ordered us food so that we did not have to leave the hospital ward. They provided us with drinks, snacks, and everything we needed so that we didn't leave Cyndy for them to watch.

After traction Cyndy needed to have casts on both feet. It didn't take her long to realize that if she soiled her cast she could get new ones. We were embarrassed every time Cyndy managed to put poop down inside the casts or rub it in on the outside. If it wasn't feces then Cyndy would put ink pens down them to scratch the itch and then get the pen stuck. Lord help us if we fed her something for dinner she didn't like because she would get rid of it by putting it down inside the cast, sometimes without us knowing until we smelled the stench. She routinely broke the plaster requiring the doctors to put on new ones. At least two to three times a week we ended up at Dr. St. Clair's office to change a cast.

We tried to make the best of it – decorating the casts first with pumpkins for Halloween and then turkeys and pumpkins for Thanksgiving. At Christmas time the casts had bright colored Christmas trees and wreaths or snowmen on them. We laughed about putting Cyndy out in the front yard with lights on. Even if we didn't have time to put up any other Christmas decorations up, we could put Cyndy outside!

Thank God in the beginning of January of 1995 we were able to finally get the casts off and get Cyndy fitted for hard plastic braces called ankle-foot orthoses (AFOs) which would give her much-needed leg support. The AFOs had a cable that ran up the back of her legs and hooked to her waist to help her get used to walking without aid. To our dismay when we asked our insurance company to cover the braces they didn't see a reason that the AFOs were needed or that they could do any good for her. They would pay for a wheelchair but not the braces because they were only "experimental" and therefore not covered as a benefit. The worst part was we didn't have the money – a couple thousand dollars! - to pay for the braces. We quickly turned to God and prayed that He would intervene and have the insurance pay for the AFOs. It took us six weeks speaking on the phone with different people in the insurance office every other day. It seemed like I was always on the phone just trying to get someone to understand my plight and have some sympathy. I knew then that we were going to have to take this particular matter up in prayer, leave it in the devoted hands of our Lord, and trust Him with the next step.

God's provision in this matter reminds me of Matthew 6:25-34:

> "Therefore I tell you, do not be anxious about your life, what you will eat, or what you will drink, nor about your body, what you will put on. Is not life more than food and the body more than clothing? Look at the birds of the air: they neither sow nor reap nor gather into barns, and yet your heavenly Father feeds them. Are you not of more value than they? And which of you by being anxious can add a single hour to his span of life? And why are you anxious about clothing? Consider the lilies of the field, how they grow: they neither toil nor spin, yet I tell you, even Solomon in all his glory was not arrayed like one of these. But if God so clothes the grass of the field, which today is alive and tomorrow is thrown into the oven, will he not much more clothe you, O you of little faith? Therefore, do not be anxious, saying, 'What shall we eat?' or 'What shall we drink?' or 'what shall we wear?' For the Gentiles seek after all these things, and your heavenly Father knows that you need them all. But seek first the kingdom of God and his righteousness, and all these things will be added to you. Therefore, do not be anxious about tomorrow, for tomorrow will be anxious for itself. Sufficient for the day is its own trouble."

We were blessed after Dr. Garrison and Dr. St. Clair wrote letters on our behalf to the insurance company and it finally paid for them!

I am slowly but surely coming to realize that there is no getting around God; He is there for me even when I do not see it. Cyndy wore the braces and they gradually improved Cyndy's walk. They made her steadier on her feet for over a year. When she had a growth spurt it made the cables too small for her and she hated wearing them. When the AFOs had gotten a little small on her, Cyndy would cry and pull them

Looking forward to another Christmas.

off. Instead of fighting with her I would give up and then Dr. White would fuss at me, asking why she didn't have them on for one of her appointments.

In the spring of 1996 we returned to Dr. St. Clair to schedule the second of Cyndy's reconstructive surgeries. Before this surgery, Cyndy had to go to the children's hospital in Richmond for a special gait/motion analysis. The doctors placed leads on Cyndy's legs, hips, and upper body to see how she walked. The computer program translated the motions into a moveable stick figure on the computer screen, where it could analyze Cyndy's weaknesses. Cyndy had to wear a two-piece bathing suit for the test. When the nurse had placed the leads too close to Cyndy's private area she smacked the nurse's hand and gave her the dirtiest look! Cyndy was acting so modest it would surprise anyone who didn't know her that she would dance nude in her bedroom window at home!

Cyndy had the second of the three surgeries on August 27, 1996. She had bilateral tibial/fibular rotational osteotomies and bilateral application of multi-planar external fixators. Cyndy did exceptionally well during the surgery and in post-op. However, the next day around noon she took a turn for the worse.

We had gone home after the surgery to get a good night's sleep before returning. We arrived the next morning to assist Cyndy with her breakfast and her bath before she fell back to sleep from the pain medication. When lunch came we woke Cyndy up to feed her but she was a little groggy. After eating she was resting peacefully so Mark and I went to get us some lunch. When we got back to the room Cyndy was not responsive. Apparently Cyndy had aspirated on her lunch and she developed a high fever that caused her to seizure and sent her into respiratory failure. Cyndy was in a full fledged code. Before Mark and I could get our wits about us the nurses were asking us if we wanted them to continue with the code or let her go. Mark and I were very upset that they were asking us if we wanted to let her go. We wanted them to do everything possible to save her life!

My heart leapt into my throat when I realized there was a possibility she could die. We were counting on Cyndy to be a fighter and pull through this; she had always bounced back after a setback very quickly. We thought she would do it again. However this time when she coded, we were not sure what was going to happen. We didn't know if she had fought her last battle. We hoped and prayed that the surgery wasn't the cause. We didn't know if maybe she had picked up a bug that caused the problem. No matter what the doctors and nurses did to help Cyndy just wasn't responding. This was the second time in a just couple of years that we almost lost her. We had the feeling that her time was coming sooner than later.

Our little Cyndy had been placed on the prayer band at our church and other churches as well. Everyone that knew about Cyndy was holding her, and us, up in prayer. Mark and I pleaded with God not to take our daughter's life. We knew there was nothing impossible with God and that He would give an ear to our prayers. Scripture reminded us that NOTHING WAS IMPOSSIBLE WITH GOD.

"With man this is impossible, but with God all things are possible." - Matthew 19:26

Although it wasn't long, time seemed to stand still. The nurses and doctors were able to resuscitate Cyndy. She was sent to the ICU for the next few days to recover from her ordeal. Having Cyndy so close to death made me fearful of leaving the hospital for any length of time. At home in the evening and night I was fearful of the phone ringing, expecting someone to say that Cyndy was taking a turn for the worse again. Mark and I prayed earnestly, on our knees, at night and in the morning, before going to the hospital that God would sustain her life for His glory. I kept reassuring myself by recalling the times before when Cyndy was so ill when Christ would put His hand upon her and she would bounce back to good health.

This was only the second of the three surgeries. Unfortunately Cyndy never made it to the last one, which was a hip repair scheduled for the next summer. I believe Cyndy wanted us to know she was ready to go home where she would be in peace forever where there would be no suffering or heartache and where she would be made whole.

We noticed that Cyndy had started to act more despondent after that episode. Her health deteriorated very rapidly afterwards. We believed she was upset with us for bringing her back to life. Perhaps during her near-death experience she saw an angel who let her know that she would be in heaven soon. We believe with all our hearts that Cyndy knew she would not have to worry about her failing body anymore when she would be with her Savior. We knew she looked forward to that glorious day when the seizures would end and she would be able to talk and walk normally.

DR. WHITE: Cyndy's 10th birthday was a day of celebration and, for me, a time of reflection. Some people hadn't given her a chance to make it one year, much less 10. At times we were thinking ahead about adjusting her schooling. I was troubled by some changes in her muscle tone, which had gotten tighter and had already led to surgical intervention by the orthopedists - no splinting, cables, and therapy could prevent worsening of her walking. While she was still having seizures we didn't have to put her in the hospital as often. Mogadon had become an orphan drug; the medication study that Cyndy was a part of did not convince the FDA enough to approve it. The drug company was very gracious about continuing it in children that had shown a good response but we all realized that would not last forever. I still had vivid memories of when the supply stock got low and even briefly ran out in the past.

Another thing that worried me was that Cyndy seemed to get sick a little easier than when she was younger. After her orthopedic surgery she developed pneumonia from aspiration. It seemed that she was developing fevers more frequently, which in turn triggered her seizures. Changing her seizure medications included adding two new medications and decreasing the

Mogadon a little, hoping that perhaps she was metabolizing it differently than when she was little. Other treatments such as the special ketogenic diet and seizure surgery were not good options and the newer medications we use today weren't available then. Fearing that she may have some worsening disorder we repeated tests looking for "storage" diseases and found nothing. Our best efforts just weren't good enough.

After the surgery, Cyndy started having more seizure spells and wasn't bouncing back as quickly as she had before. The thought of Cyndy dying was become more of a reality. I started slipping into depression. I didn't have the energy or will power to do anything except take care of Cyndy. I couldn't clean my house or keep on top of things. My house fell into a state of utter disaster. I felt sheer hopelessness anticipating Cyndy's impending death. I wasn't bothered about how my house looked or what people assumed when they saw it. If they didn't like the way the house looked they could do something to make it better or leave me alone.

The day before Thanksgiving I got the courage to ask Dr. White if Cyndy was dying. His expression told me everything. My first clue something was amiss was when he turned away from me for several minutes; when he turned back around his eyes were watering and tears were streaking down his face. He was slow to speak; he was looking for the words to soften the blow. His actions and concerns confirmed for me that Cyndy's life was ending soon. My absolute worst fears for my daughter were coming true; the news was more than either one of us could bear...

DR. WHITE: The day we nearly lost Cyndy after the surgery I had a very uncomfortable feeling. Her health was rapidly going downhill. I wasn't sure what other medications we could try at this point; we had gone through all the possible medications and even tried a few again hoping to control Cyndy's seizures but with no success. I had many restless nights worrying silently about what else I could do for Cyndy. Her seizures were becoming more violent and each episode was lasting longer. I questioned Anne often to make sure she had enough emergency medication for Cyndy's seizures. To complicate matters Cyndy was having a harder time fighting off viruses that were going around that fall and winter. I constantly warned Anne to be on watch for signs and symptoms that Cyndy was becoming sick. The more quickly she noticed changes in Cyndy's health the better chance she would have to pull through.

I warned Mark and Anne to be extra careful during the winter months, which is a time that neurologists worry about, usually silently. The effects of the nasty flu and other infections can be catastrophic to our disabled population. As Christmas came again my prayers turned to

No corner could contain her!

Cyndy – that she and all of my other young patients would experience a holiday season free of illness and accident.

Following Dr. White's advice, I was constantly watching Cyndy for any signs or symptoms of illness. There were times when I would put her to bed and she would be well but then during the night her health would change quickly. Things seemed to start changing for the worse right at Christmas; Cyndy's health alarmed both Dr. White and Dr. Garrison. Something was happening with Cyndy. We prayed for Cyndy's health but she was sliding further downhill and quickly.

> Prayer:
> Thank you God for the lessons we implicitly learn through the most trying times in our lives. Thank you for being there to generously assist us in making the right decisions even when it's painful to follow You. Thank you for Your everlasting faithfulness.
> In Christ,
> Amen

CHAPTER ELEVEN

I Will Come Again, and Receive You Unto Myself

""Let not your hearts be troubled. Believe in God; believe also in me. In my Father's house are many rooms. If it were not so, would I have told you that I go to prepare a place for you? And if I go and prepare a place for you, I will come again and will take you to myself, that where I am you may be also. And you know the way to where I am going."
- John 14:1-4

The week in between Christmas and New Year's Cyndy had been having non-stop seizures. Once we got the seizures under control with valium just four to six hours later she would have another seizure. Looking back on that last week I can see how Cyndy was trying to say good-bye numerous times. She was pleading for us to let her go to be with the Lord.

On Christmas Eve when Cyndy woke up from her nap she came down the stairs and started to go into seizure. She fell half way down the stairs. We tried not to let it worry us but we were unnerved; something was not right. We called Dr. Garrison who encouraged us to not worry but keep a careful eye on her and watch for signs of any potential head injury problems. Cyndy didn't appear to be feeling bad other than being a little bit slower than normal and not getting into the festivities

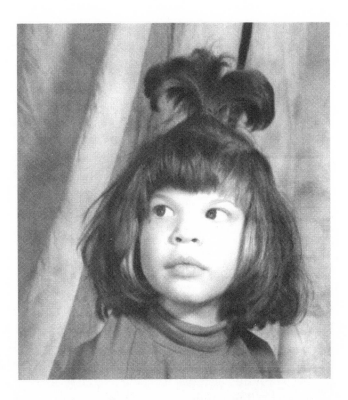

going on around her, but she bounced back as the day went on.

On Christmas Eve Cyndy wanted to go for a walk outside. I took her up and down the street looking at the lights. She stopped me and pointed upward toward the heavens. She was cooing and pointing like she was trying to tell me something. I realized a week later that she was telling me that she would be going to be with the Lord soon.

That night at the Christmas Eve service, Cyndy was sitting beside me. She seemed to really enjoy the Christmas music. Barbara, a lady from church, told me later that she was listening to Cyndy sing on Christmas Eve. Barbara said that Cyndy was singing in key and she understood every word Cyndy sang. I did not hear what Barbara heard. I just heard Cyndy cooing loudly.

Christmas morning Cyndy didn't care to open any of her presents. It was as if she was telling us that she didn't need them because she wasn't going to be here to play with them. My nephew Jay was carrying her around up at my parents. He was the only one she was responding to; he was the only one who could get her to eat a little. Soon she began

Cyndy withi Santa Claus (Daddy) at the Infant Stem Christmas party.

convulsing. They weren't bad enough for a trip to the hospital, so I quickly called Dr. White.

While talking with Dr. White he reminded me what he had said just a month earlier. He had already used all the available medications for Cyndy. He ordered some levels to be drawn the next day to see if he could add another drug to her protocol. Before he hung up, he said for us to enjoy the holiday since we couldn't know what was coming next year. Deep down I knew he was right. I knew her time was going by quickly; I knew that soon she would be healed in eternity. The levels that Dr. White had drawn would come back a week later and haunt him.

While the rest of the world celebrated New Year's Eve we were sitting in a hospital waiting room on account of some health issues I was having. When Cyndy got up out of the chair and walked over to me she walked perfectly straight. She was not bent over; she was very steady on her feet. What a beautiful awe-inspiring blessing to see her walk over to me like a normal, healthy young woman. She walked as if she never had a problem with her legs or back! I believe God was most graciously giving us a glimpse of Cyndy in heaven. She would soon be walking, talking, and completely free of seizures. The most important blessing - the best of all we could ask - is that she would be in the arms of our sweet Savior and walking and talking up a storm.

We went out to eat at the Golden Corral that evening for dinner and surprisingly Cyndy wanted me to feed her. I was surprised since she had not asked, or wanted anyone, to feed her in years! Looking back, I feel remorseful for getting upset with her for wanting me to feed her. That was the last time I had a chance to feed her. Even now I still feel a heavy sense of guilt that I did not cherish every moment with Cyndy on her last day. It could have been filled with memories and no regrets when she went to be with Jesus. If I only knew that she was going home to her heavenly Father so soon I would have fed her all of that meal and more.

The night before Cyndy died she was laying on the sofa sleeping rather peacefully like she was listening to something. When Mark went to move Cyndy up to her bed she acted as if she really didn't want to be moved from the sofa. Cyndy seemed to be in another world, a land of awe. Did Cyndy hear the angels singing her to sleep? Were choir of angels already descending from Heaven to earth and ascending back to Heaven ushering her into the arms of Jesus? Did she know her days and maybe hours were ending soon? Had she been trying to tell us something earlier that day while in the waiting room at the hospital—"look at how straight I'm walking and standing?"

I believe Cyndy knew that the Lord was coming for her in the still of the night ever since August when she nearly went home after her surgery. Perhaps Cyndy knew every single precise song that the angels were singing to her that night; I can only imagine the sounds of the harps, and trumpets, along with other stringed instruments being played by the angels – perhaps even musical instruments that we haven't even heard of here on this earth! Just contemplating how each musical instrument must be played so meticulously, nothing off beat or off-key...thousands of members in the orchestra...WOW!

"And suddenly there was with the angel a multitude of the heavenly host praising God, and saying, Glory to God in the highest, and on earth peace, good will toward men." - Luke 2:13-14

"And I heard a voice from heaven, as the voice of many waters, and as the voice of a great thunder: and I heard the voice of harpers harping with their harps. And they sung as it were a new song before the throne, and before the four beasts, and the elders: and no man could learn that song but the hundred and forty and four thousand, which were redeemed from the earth." - Rev. 14:2-3

I can only envision how beautiful the choir of angels must have sounded to Cyndy and all our other Christian family members and friends that have gone before her. I know the angelic choirs must have been spectacular beyond what we can see or hear here on earth!

On New Year's morning 1997, just after nine-thirty in the morning, Mark found Cyndy's lifeless body in her bed. The night before he had tucked her snugly in beside Katie and Joel at the top of the bed. However during the night some time she had moved to the foot of the bed. Perhaps she saw Jesus standing at the door of her room and went into His arms, but she couldn't take her exhausted body. She had died peacefully in her sleep sometime in the early morning hours; her precious sprit had returned to her Heavenly Father.

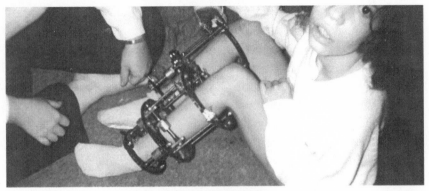

Cyndy's last surgery.

When Mark realized that Cyndy was dead he called me to her room. I stood there in sheer shock. I felt frozen. I was in denial that Cyndy would ever die...there was no way that one of my children would die. Mark tried to get through to me, as gently as possible, that our daughter had left us. Something inside me broke loose. I became hysterical. I was screaming at the top of my lungs, crying, and pushing Mark away from me. I did not want to believe Cyndy had left us. I scooped Cyndy up in my arms and ran downstairs. I placed her on the floor and began doing CPR. I could see that she wasn't breathing and that I was going to have to give her mouth to mouth and start compressions to get her heart beating.

I prayed the whole time I was administering CPR on Cyndy that this would be the one time CPR would work on someone – that it would bring her back. On the other hand, maybe Cyndy wasn't really dead...we were just in some sort of horrible nightmare and when we woke up Cyndy would be still be alive and with us. When we would wake up Cyndy would be doing her usual... NO SHE'S NOT DEAD, NO NO! What made it so hard for all of us to believe that she was dead was that Cyndy was a fighter and when you thought she would be down and out she wouldn't be.

It was when I started CPR that I noticed her hands were fixed; rigor mortis had already set in. I heard a voice say, "Leave her alone now that she is Mine!" and all of a sudden I noticed that my hands were being clapped together forcefully, as if Cyndy was telling me that she was better now, the seizure was over for good. The huge, heavy burden that was always on shoulders – my worry over Cyndy's seizures - was gone forever. I knew that Cyndy was in better hands and that she was not in pain anymore. Joy washed over me. Right then I knew then that she could walk and talk normally now, like a healthy child. I began praising

God for looking after Cyndy and for the 11 short years He had given us with her. Part of me was happy she was home with the Lord, yet another part of me was immensely sad that she was no longer here with us.

My heart eased for a while. I realized the ultimate decision was made. There was no more that I could do. I kept reminding myself that deep down I was glad that Cyndy would no longer have to worry about another seizure. Her legs would never give out on her again. Best of all now she was able to speak! But the other part of me did not want to let my little girl go, no matter how bad off she was...I wanted her no matter what condition she was in.

"He will wipe away every tear from their eyes, and death shall be
no more, neither shall there be mourning nor crying nor pain anymore,
for the former things have passed away." - Rev. 21:4

My prayers had been heard. The weight on my shoulders was lifted. She was made perfect in the presence of God.

I knew Cyndy's personality and life here on earth was gone forever. Memories of Cyndy were all I would have left to get me through the rest of my days of my life. Cyndy left this cruel sinful world behind and had entered into the peacefulness of Heaven where she would see that the restraints she had here are of the past. As for Mark and I, we would not have to worry about seeing her seizure ever again. Those ordeals were gone and would be buried in the grave with her never to be seen again. The illnesses that plagued her for her 11 years of her life could no longer get her down... her life was changed in a twinkle of the eye...there would not be any pain caused from her weak legs ever again. When she closed her eyes here on earth she woke in Heaven with the Lord where there would not be sickness or death. Those things had passed away. She was now forever in the arms of Jesus, singing His praises all day and night long.

Once the emergency crew was called our family was sent into turmoil. Our house was filled with police, with investigators taking pictures and dusting for fingerprints, with social services workers, and friends and family rushing to help. In the madness my ability to think rationally had long been lost. A confused and surprised hurt that felt more like numbness gave way over the day to a sad and angry hurt that blurred my vision, gripped my stomach, and crushed my chest. My daughter, my angel... was gone. All I could do was wish that God had taken me instead and feel angrier that He had not.

I became extremely furious with my husband for putting Cyndy in her bed instead of leaving her downstairs where she was sleeping so soundly. WHY DIDN'T WE - FOR THE LOVE OF GOD - HAVE KEPT CYNDY DOWN STAIRS WITH US?! WE WOULD HAVE KNOWN SOMETHING WAS WRONG WITH HER! IF ONLY... one of us had checked on her during the night, anticipating another seizure...we could have done something and just maybe...she would still be alive...If only I could have done something... to stop Cyndy from dying, maybe she would still be here today...this gaping hole in our hearts would not be festering as a painful boil about to erupt spewing its poison.

It does no good to entertain the thoughts of "if only." In hindsight our "if only" can never change what has already happened. As Dr. White would tell me when I look back "going back will not UNBREAK the glass window that has already been broken." We cannot predict the future, nor change the past. Only God knows every solitary event that will happen in our life before we are yet to be put upon this earth. No matter what the outcome will be, we can never outsmart God. The Lord knows the number of stars in the sky even their names, the hairs on our head, and the number of seconds we will be on this earth, before He calls us home to be with Him.

> "If I would count them, they are more than the sand. I awake, and I am still with you." - Psalm 139:18

> "He determines the number of the stars; he gives to all of them their names." - Psalm 147:4

> "But even the hairs of your head are all numbered." - Matthew 10:30

> "Why, even the hairs of your head are all numbered. Fear not; you are of more value than many sparrows." - Luke 12:7

As for me, I needed to put Cyndy into the hands of Christ and let the Lord's will be done. I needed to be like what the Bible recorded when God gave Solomon his wisdom.

> "And God gave Solomon wisdom and understanding beyond measure, and breadth of mind like the sand on the seashore, so that Solomon's wisdom surpassed the wisdom of all the people of the east and all the wisdom of Egypt." - 1 Kings 4:29-30

Most parents' response to losing a child is denial. I didn't want to believe Dr. White when he told me that Cyndy would probably die young. Even when he told me on Christmas Day that he thought her time was getting near I wanted him to be wrong. Losing a child is something that happens to other people, never me! I have had family members who lost children but it could never happen to me! There had been so many times in the 11 years that Cyndy cheated death...where she came so close to dying but then somehow with the help of the Lord she pulled through and had gotten better.

DR. WHITE: Although Anne swears that I had told her that Cyndy would die, I really don't remember saying anything to anyone about the way she had recovered from her orthopedic surgery earlier that fall. I was also worried that the seizure frequency had increased and we had run out of new options, but with a new year coming the chance of new medications was possible, and I was obviously worried about her getting sick. As her first decade ended we actually began wondering what things would be like as she continued to grow. But now that was all gone. And I felt awful.

It was very painful when the funeral home arrived to remove Cyndy's body. Reality set in. Cyndy would never walk through the front door never again. Seeing the hearse backing up to our house and watching the attendants pull out a stretcher from the back of the hearse and enter our home knowing they had came for Cyndy...my baby really was gone. When they picked up Cyndy off the floor with the sheet still draped over her and placed her on the stretcher--and then draped another cover over her...I felt like my heart was being torn from my chest. I wanted to yell..."NO...LEAVE CYNDY ALONE ...she is my daughter and you cannot take her... please just go away and leave us alone...NO PLEASE TAKE THAT SHEET OFF HER FACE... she is not dead; she is still alive! THIS CAN'T BE HAPPENING TO US... GOD... PLEASE let me wake up and this cannot be true! OH GOD WHY??? WHY GOD WHY???"

I was so overwhelmed grief that I collapsed as Cyndy was being carried out of the house. The police thought that I had had a seizure and called the rescue squad back to give me medical attention. But no medical attention could help me...I just wanted my daughter back. In my despair I wished they could put me in the casket with Cyndy.

Right after the funeral home hearse left social services began removing our other five children from our home. The police alleged that my negligence had caused Cyndy's death. The authorities argued that I should have left Cyndy in her bed and that by moving her I had placed her in additional danger. I was stunned. How dare they accuse me of hurting Cyndy! She had already died when we found her in bed. How dare they judge my actions! What would they have done if it was their child that had been found dead? They would have moved her and tried to do CPR until they realized that she was gone. It had only been a day shy of a week since Jonbenèt Ramsey was found dead. The police probably thought they had a similar case on their hands, since I was severely depressed.

The police and social services staff marched the children right past their deceased sister's body. Mark and I were not allowed to touch them or say anything to them. The social services staff and police were adding trauma on top of trauma. As the children were being taken I began to wonder if there was really a God. If so, why would a loving God who is so good let us lose one child to death then pull the other five children away from us? Where was He? Just an hour earlier I had felt the arms of God around me letting me know that Cyndy was safe and that she was in His haven of rest but now, when my other children were being removed from our care, I couldn't understand why He was hurting me so badly. I wanted to reject Him. He did not act like a loving Father to me; He was a hateful father and why would I care about a God that just puts more hurt and anger in my life? I went from loving God as a Lord to hating him and anything to do with him in a matter of minutes. I wasn't sure what I felt anymore. Yet still the truth remained that God knew what I was feeling and loved me no matter how I acted toward Him that day.

After the police left our house Dr. Garrison called us. He heard that Cyndy had passed and wanted to get some of her doctors to be pallbearers. The reality was sinking in. He said he would call Dr. White. He told us to get Cyndy's funeral arrangements taken care of and leave the worry of getting our other children back to him and Dr. White. We knew the state was already questioning if someone killed Cyndy and, if so, who? Knowing the state's concerns made funeral arrangements seem even harder.

DR. WHITE: When I got the call from Dr. Garrison that Cyndy had been found dead in her bed, it revived memories of the near miss events she had, had years earlier, and raised all the questions that we had sorted through before. Had she been sick? Was it SUDS? Aspiration? Smothering? We had been checking blood levels and blood tests, and they were acceptable, she had not had any fevers, and I knew that her family had been watchful. Perhaps--- it was just was meant to be.... After all those years....it was good-bye.

The calls kept coming. The call from Dr. Garrison that the other kids had been removed from the home. Then the call from the coroner's office wondering why the blood levels of her anticonvulsants were so high; I had recently checked them in the hospital lab and they were high normal but not toxic.

Now I was really sick.

Did I misjudge Anne? Was she capable of overdosing her daughter? Did I contribute in some way? Was it something I did, something I missed, something I should have done? How much contact should I have with the grieving family? Would I get in the way of finding out what happened? Do they even want to see me?

Social Services left and we had to think about going to the funeral home to begin planning for Cyndy's burial. It was the hardest thing Mark and I had to do. We couldn't deny that Cyndy was dead when we got to the funeral home. We had to come to terms that it was not a nightmare - it was really happening to us. Cyndy was dead and now we had to pick out a casket and vault and plan what kind of service we wanted for her. Several times I got out of the car and then climbed right back in pleading with my parents, my brother Jimmy, and Mark not to make me go in the funeral home. I was in a daze. The shock of death was becoming reality; my worst fear was taking place.

Walking inside the funeral home gave me a sick feeling in my stomach. Parents should not have to plans a funeral for their child. Going into the casket room and seeing all the caskets was so painful. This final thing we could do for Cyndy now was to pick out something that Cyndy would be buried in. This was the start of the whirlwind of all the final things to come over the next couple days...how were we going to deal with the funeral and actual burial? How could we put our daughter in a casket and close the lid? My Dad was so full of grief that he wanted the very best casket that was in the room – an expensive Oakwood casket. Just to hurry up and get out of that room we went along with his decision. We left the casket room and tried to figure out a payment plan.

Jimmy told us to rethink that choice. It was a lot of money – money that we were putting in the ground and would never see again once she was buried. The thing Mark and I had to remember was that Cyndy was not there in that casket. That body in the casket was just her shell; what made Cyndy had gone to be with the Lord. We both believe that when we die, our bodies turn back to dust, and our souls are what keep living either with the Lord or in hell.

> *"By the sweat of your face you shall eat bread, till you return to the ground, for out of it you were taken; for you are dust, and to dust you shall return." - Genesis 3:19*

We went back into the room again. It was hard but we were able to pick a cheaper casket. We did everything as quickly as we could to leave the funeral home and deal with everything else that had taken place that day.

Now that the casket and vault were picked out, we needed to get her body from the state to have her prepared for burial. The funeral director had to call the state several times to get them to release Cyndy's body to be prepared. Next it was getting a dress that would look good on Cyndy; one that would make her look like a young woman instead of that childish Cyndy she once was. Cyndy was not one for wearing dresses; she usually wore pants since they would keep her diapers covered and made it more difficult for her to take the diaper off. We thought it would be difficult to pick out a dress but we found a beautiful burgundy dress in the teen section; it made her look older then her age and very mature. Seeing her in that beautiful dress she no longer looked like an immature handicapped child; she looked like a very mature normal young woman. Perhaps God was showing us how beautiful His servant Cyndy was looking in Heaven, since Christ promises us that our imperfections here on earth are made right when we see Christ. In the presence of the Lord, Cyndy walks and talks perfectly with Christ!

After we finished all the funeral arrangements that could be made for that day, our next question was where were our other five children? Where had the social services placed the older boys? With all their special needs we knew they would be very hard to place in a foster home. We figured they may have been placed in a hospital somewhere. Mark and I hoped that Social Services would have placed Katie and Joel together since they were easier to place and that perhaps they would not be as traumatized about being removed from the home after experiencing the death or their sister if they were together.

At least we knew the children would be safe for the next few days as we got through Cyndy's funeral. Then we could face head-on the problems that were waiting us with our other five children. They were never far from our thoughts; we worried about what they were thinking and would we ever get them back? We knew it was going to take an act of Congress to get the children back. We needed to place that fight in the hands of Drs. Garrison and White since they had asked we leave that part up to them. Ultimately our burden was placed on the shoulders of our Heavenly Father. Only He could change things and have the children returned.

We went to my parents' house that night. My mother was stern with family members and friends that came to visit. When she felt we had enough visitors she started to usher them out the door. Before going to sleep I took a walk outside around my parents' garden. As I walked I was talking with the Lord. I was looking for the brightest star in the sky, for that night Cyndy was resting in the arms of Jesus. First, the grief of Cyndy's death and then having all of our other children being taken from us...how in the world were we going to be able to put one foot in front of the other?! Only God could help us get through the stress of a funeral....God alone!

We were given sleeping pills to get us through the first night. At times we fought the meds. Laying my head on the pillow and closing my eyes I kept replaying the scene of Cyndy's dead body lying in front of me. I was afraid of what tomorrow would bring. Mark and I were completely broken.

Prayer:
Thank you Lord for loving us when we act so foolishly before we stop and look and see what you have in store for us. Thank you for holding us tight in your arms when we hurt. Thank you for understanding that in our time of greatest need all we really need is you. Thank you for watching over us in the valley shadow of death, for thou art with us.
In Christ's Name,
Amen

CHAPTER TWELVE

A Celebration of Cyndy's Life in God's Glory

"I have said these things to you, that in me you may have peace.
In the world you will have tribulation. But take heart; I have overcome
the world." - John 16:33

On Friday January 3rd, the day before the funeral, we had to go and view Cyndy's remains. Mark and I weren't prepared to see Cyndy being motionless...lifeless. It was sobering to see her in the casket. It had been a long two days since the funeral home had taken her body to the medical examiner's office. To protect ourselves from further pain we had not yet really admitted that Cyndy wasn't ever coming back home. However once we stood before her, laid out in a casket, we could no longer refute that she was dead. We had to admit and come to terms that Cyndy was not with us here on earth.

The shock of seeing her lying still in a casket and unresponsive was mind-boggling. This nightmare is true...SHE'S GONE! As I stood there the room started turning dark, my legs were starting to feel tingly and weak, and I realized that I was going to pass out from shock of seeing our daughter laid out in a casket. We could not believe that she had passed on to the Lord and that we would never be able to see or touch her anymore in our lifetime. Cyndy had been feeling fairly well the day before she died and now all of a sudden she was no longer here. Standing there not hearing her clapping or cooing we just could not believe the child we were viewing was our Cyndy our oldest daughter. We were so devastated. We just stood there looking at Cyndy and then back at each other. We wanted so much to grab Cyndy by the shoulders, shake her, and shout at her to wake up and let's get out of here, none of us wanted to be here in this funeral home. COME ON CYNDY PLEASE WAKE UP...LET'S GET OUT OF HERE ...IT IS NO TIME FOR PLAYING NOW CYNDY...COME ON CYNDY PLEASE GET UP!

Cyndy looked so different than when she died. That New Year's morning we could tell by her color and how her hands had set in rigor mortis that she had a seizure and her airway had collapsed causing her death; here in the casket however she did not have the bluish color any longer. She appeared to be very peaceful. The funeral home had fixed her up to look like a princess, like a normal teenager, or more so a bride going to meet her husband. She just looked like she had fallen asleep and woke in HEAVEN WALKING SIDE BY SIDE WITH THE LORD.

After we stood there viewing her body for a few minutes, we had gathered our wits about ourselves and wound up her beloved Pooh bear one last time. We were looking at the flowers. About 15 minutes passed when unexpectedly the yellow bear that had stopped playing a month before began to play "Jesus Loves Me." Maybe the angels had wound the yellow teddy bear up to let us know that Cyndy was at rest in the arms of Jesus and she was talking up a storm.

Mark and I stood there and looked at each other in shock while the bear played. A feeling of peacefulness came over us; we knew in our hearts that our Cyndy was telling us that she was completely well again and at peace with the Lord. The body in that casket was not the real Cyndy. It was just a shell, the real Cyndy ran, not walked, to her Lord.

I began thinking about how Cyndy was handicapped...and how her bear was broken. Tossing the bear in the trash would have been like how some of my family had rejected Cyndy. As I reflected on the love that Christ had for Cyndy I realized how intense the love Christ has for all of us. I realized that she had been made handicapped and died early for a reason, so that we might bring honor and praise to the Lord even when we are hurting. A month before she died that yellow teddy bear that she loved so much stopped playing. Cyndy became very distraught that her teddy bear friend could no longer play "Jesus Loves Me" to her. She was inconsolable even when we gave her another bear to take its place. Broken or not that yellow bear was her pride and joy. She would bring that bear to us to be wound up even when we had told her that it was broken. She would cry when we handed it back to her. When Christmas came, her last Christmas with us, Cyndy had been given a Pooh bear that also played "Jesus Loves Me," but it just was different to her. She wanted a cuddy yellow bear like the one she had, or she wanted her soft yellow bear fixed.

Even with the assurance of God's grace in our hearts, we were overwhelmed with sorrow. We tried to find solace in an article my brother-in-law, the Rev. William Harrell, wrote entitled *"Godly Joy and Godly Sorrow."*

> *"It is true that Scripture declares the joy of the Lord to be our strength. However, Jesus also declares that those who mourn are blessed with divine comfort. (Mt.5:4) 'Blessed are those who mourn, for they shall be comforted.' The Apostle Paul writes about the considerable benefits of godly sorrow (2Cor. 7:11), 'For see what earnestness this godly grief has produced in you, but also what eagerness to clear yourselves, what indignation, what fear, what longing, what zeal, what punishment! At every point you have proved yourselves innocent in the matter.' ...while the writer of the Hebrews teaches us not to despise the discipline of the Lord that makes us sorrowful for a season, but afterward yields the peaceful fruit of righteousness (Heb. 12:11) 'For the moment all discipline seems painful rather than pleasant, but later it yields the peaceful fruit of righteousness to those who have been trained by it.' ...Our Westminster Confession of Faith makes clear to us that joy comes as the end of man's being perfected by the gracious, redeeming, and sanctifying work of God. It is man's chief end that he should enjoy God forever. Here in our earthly pilgrimage, godly sorrow is a much more constant companion and sure guide for the believer. Far from our seeking at all times to make ourselves happy we are called to humble ourselves under God's mighty hand, knowing that He will exalt us at the proper time." (1 Peter 5:6) "Humble yourselves, therefore, under the mighty hand of God so that at the proper time he may exalt you,"*

Saturday January 4th, 1997 was a very sad day for us. As we were getting into our car to leave for Cyndy's funeral service at Calvary Presbyterian Church we spotted two of the most beautiful mourning doves on rooftop of our house looking down at us; it felt like a sign from Cyndy that everything was going to be fine. Peace flowed over me. We knew that whatever happened in the next few hours, days, and weeks, we would get through with the help of God, and God alone. We needed to put our hands into the Jesus' hands, and if we would be still and let the Lord have control over the circumstances that we were in we would find the peace to get through the most painful next two and half hours of our lives.

"Whoever believes in me, as the Scripture has said, 'Out of his heart will flow rivers of living water.'" - John 7:38

"Peace I leave with you; my peace I give to you. Not as the world gives do I give to you. Let not your hearts be troubled, neither let them be afraid." - John 14:27

As the hour of Cyndy's funeral approached we wished we could turn back time. Neither Mark nor I wanted to enter the church or see our daughter's casket lying before us. Cyndy's funeral felt like our day of reckoning.

Our hearts were breaking as we entered the church knowing in a few minutes her casket would close for good, NEVER to be opened again... PLEASE STOP DON"T CLOSE THAT CASKET! STOP THAT MY DAUGHTER, STOP NO...oh no...PLEASE! Just entering the church for Cyndy's funeral was very taxing on us; if only we could have put the funeral off for a little longer.

Before going into the chapel to see Cyndy for the last time we went into the library where all the pallbearers were waiting. We wanted to pin a small carnation on each of them and thank them. Three of the pallbearers were her doctors whom had all taken splendid care of her while she was living. Two of the other pallbearers were family members (an uncle and a cousin) and the last was an elder at our church. As I entered the room all eyes were on me. They wanted to see how well I was holding up. Talking with them helped us forget for a short time what we were there to do.

Walking back into the sanctuary and toward Cyndy's casket Mark and I both knew as it would be the last time we could touch our daughter's head and hands and kiss her on her forehead. It would be the very last time on this earth we would touch her or see her. Saying bye to Cyndy was very hard to do. Memories of when she was born, when she had her near-death crises, the funny things she would do such as dancing in the window nude...all we had left were memories to make us smile when we would feel down over her death. Standing in front

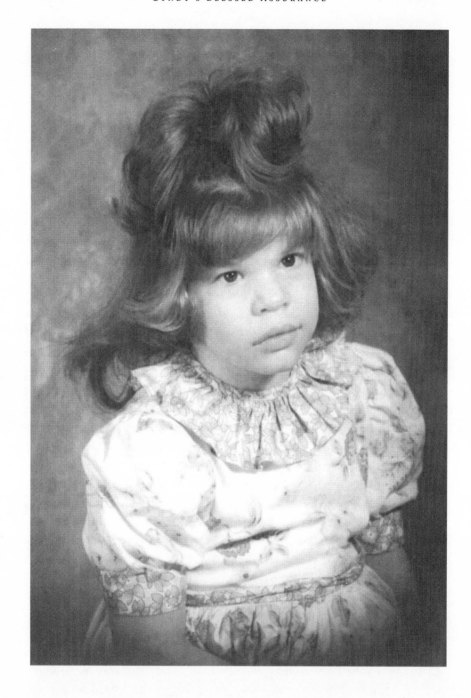

of Cyndy memories flashed before me. All I could do was cry and grip the casket. I was in agony. All I wanted to do was climb in the casket beside her and let the funeral director close it with me inside. Mark and a couple of family members tried to get me to go to the Sunday school room where the rest of the family members were waiting for the funeral to begin so the casket could be closed. I didn't want to go. I protested. I wasn't ready to say goodbye. My heart was breaking and there was nothing that could console me then. I was screaming and grabbing at the casket just to hug Cyndy one last time, to get one more view at my beautiful daughter. My hysteria made Mark and his Dad think that I was going to pull the casket, and Cyndy, down on the floor. They were finally able to pull me away.

Watching the casket being closed as we exited the sanctuary was one of my most painful memories. Since the funeral home was anxious to get on with the service they had already started to close the casket after my nephew Jay pulled the blankets up on Cyndy and wound her pooh bear up one last time. I knew when we walked back in for the service the casket would be closed. I pleaded with Mark and our pastor to please let the casket stay open during the service. But they both felt that service would be easier on me without the casket being open during the service. They also felt that an open casket would be a distraction to family and friends instead of being able to stop and listen and gain comfort from Pastor Bender's message.

The service was entitled "A Celebration of Life: Cynthia Anne Harrell." As we entered the sanctuary, the organist Jean Sullivan played "How Great Thou Art" and then "Amazing Grace." We were able to quiet our souls enough to listen to Pastor Mark's share comforting words from the Bible.

"A Psalm of David. The Lord is my shepherd; I shall not want. He makes me lie down in green pastures. He leads me beside still waters. He restores my soul. He leads me in paths of righteousness for his name's sake. Even though I walk through the valley of the shadow of death, I will fear no evil, for you are with me; your rod and your staff, they comfort me. You prepare a table before me; in the presence of my enemies; you anoint my head with oil; my cup overflows. Surely goodness and mercy shall follow me all the days of my life, and I shall dwell in the house of the Lord forever." - Psalm 23:1-6

"On the seventh day the child died. And the servants of David

If Cyndy wasn't carrying around her yellow bear she was carrying around a blanket.

were afraid to tell him that the child was dead, for they said, 'Behold, while the child was yet alive, we spoke to him, and he did not listen to us. How then can we say to him the child is dead? He may do himself some harm.' But when David saw that his servants were whispering together, David understood that the child was dead. And David said to his servants, 'Is the child dead?' They said, 'He is dead.' Then David arose from the earth and washed and anointed himself and changed his clothes. And he went into the house of the Lord and worshiped. He then went to his own house. And when he asked, they set food before him, and he ate. Then his servants said to him, 'What is this thing that you have done? You fasted and wept for the child while he was alive; but when the child died, you arose and ate food.' He said, 'While the child was still alive, I fasted and wept, for I said, 'Who knows whether the Lord will be gracious to me, that the child may live?' But now he is dead. Why should I fast? Can I bring him back again? I shall go to him, but he will not return to me.'" - 2 Samuel 12:18-23*

"I can do all things through him who strengthens me."
- Philippians 4:13

After the scripture reading Pastor Bender prayed:

"Author of life and conqueror of death we give thanks for the gift of life you gave to us in Cyndy. We pray for your comfort to attend Mark and Anne – their family, family members and relatives and others who have worked with Cyndy and loved her. Gracious God who has given us a Savior in the person of Jesus Christ our Lord. Even as He died for sin and rose from the grave. Thank you for the assurance that those who have and die in Christ shall be raised. Grant us your strength. In Christ's Name, Amen."

We were able to stop and hear the assurance that our Cyndy was with God. We filled the time with all of Cyndy's favorite hymns: "Amazing Grace," "How Great Thou Art," "Jesus Loves Me," and "This Is My Father's World." As we listened quietly Dr. Charles Kollar came over and knelt down in front of me and told us the meaning of the song "It Is Well with My Soul." He had told us that one day we would be able to say it is well with my soul when life would slow down, and we could come to grips with losing Cyndy.

Thinking back to the day Cyndy was buried, the music and the scripture that was used were such a comfort. It has left me thinking about Cyndy and the last two verses of "Blessed Assurance."

"Perfect submission, perfect delight, visions of rapture now burst on my sight... Angels descending bring from above... echoes of mercy whispers of love... This is my story, this is my song, Praise my Savior all the day long... This is my story this is my song..."

Cyndy is no longer in pain nor is she having seizures. She can speak now and her legs are no longer weak. God has had nothing but pure mercy and love for Cyndy. The love the Lord has for Cyndy we cannot comprehend, and we will not grasp until the day we are called home.

Thoughts of Cyndy now being at rest...

"perfect submission, all is at rest... (Awesome) I and my Savior are happy and blest... (Oh yes we are... how awesome knowing that Cyndy is with her Savior...) watching and waiting... (The thoughts of that my Savior is coming back for me one day... I know not only will I be with my Savior I will see my daughter again...) looking above, (I am) filled with His goodness, lost in His Love." God has watched over me and has dried my tears many of times.

Hearing Pastor Bender share the Scripture passage where King David lost his precious son brought us comfort. Knowing that a great Biblical figure like David suffered this same kind of loss and grief touched us. Pastor Bender also reminded us that Cyndy was eating at Jesus' table now, that He had prepared a banquet for her! Cyndy will never be shunned or looked down upon because of her handicaps anymore because now she has a glorified body without defect! Not only had Cyndy been made perfect in heaven but she was now the beloved daughter sitting with her King.

Pastor Bender's closing prayer also reflected the hope we know is true:

> "We give thanks, Father, that you have included children in your covenant family. Thank you for your faithful and kind love. We give thanks that in this world we are aliens and strangers. Moreover, when we depart from here, we go to a place where there is no more crying, where you wipe away our tears, where there is no more sickness or death, only joy in your glorious presence. Comfort those here today, and let our hope be found in you and in your Son Jesus, who is the only way to you, our Father. O Lord, we are all as prodigals, and we pray that you might give us the desire to return home that we might enjoy a life of nearness to you. Amen."

DR. WHITE: Pastor Mark had never eulogized a child before, they tell me; it didn't show at all. Celebrating Cyndy's life and feeling a familiar ache in my gut and chest that was relieved by, of all thing, singing hymns, made me dizzy either with hyperventilation or relief.

As the funeral services closed for Cyndy we rose to take her to her final resting place at Rosewood Cemetery in Virginia Beach, Va. The pallbearers - Dr. Larry White, her neurologist; Dr. Bobby Garrison, her primary pediatrician; and Dr. Tony Thomas her pediatrician, - carried her casket out of the funeral home. Another one of Cyndy's doctors, Dr. Victor Mickunas, wanted to serve as a pallbearer but couldn't because he had duty. He managed to arrive at the funeral in time to greet us at the back of the church and kiss Cyndy's casket before we left. It was a rare and unique gift to have Cyndy's doctors not only attend her funeral but also want to be an integral part of the service. Each one of them wanted to do something for Cyndy since she showed them so much love. They loved her dearly and truly grieved her passing. The other three pallbearers were my nephew Jay Harrison, Cyndy's Uncle Brian Morris, and Eddie Sullivan, an elder in our church.

DR. WHITE: Cyndy's funeral was as stressful as I knew it would be, and I was worried about Anne's mental health. As I met family members and church members, I noticed that all her pediatric doctors were there and they wanted to do something for her that I had not seen nor heard of until then—we all served as her pallbearers. Of the few memories I have of that day the most vivid one is how heavy that coffin was. Cyndy had always been so light to carry; no trouble at all really. It was then that I realized that it wasn't the coffin that was heavy...it was my heart.

There are a lot of reasons people go to funerals, and a likely equal number that people don't go: personal loss (or gain, if they read the will), family support (or lack of), saying goodbye, paying respect, and many others. If you are a physician you add a few more. It is tempting for someone who has taken an oath to preserve and enrich life to view a funeral as a failing, personal or systematic. But life is precious and temporary, and while we medical types have to come up with ways to extend and enhance life for patients young and old, we can't change that.

In my case there is another fairly powerful motivation at work. Since childhood a progressive anxiety disorder has made life's choices difficult for me: while making it through college and med school were possible with youthful energy and compulsive overachievement, and as an adult I can avoid meetings, movies, plays, concerts, large congregations of people and excess noise, there are times that I just have to suck it up and be there for my patients and/or their families (weddings and graduations are big). Other people can have success managing their anxiety with medications, hypnosis, and behavioral therapy; it didn't work for me.

So I knew I had to go to the funeral.

Despite Anne's assurances when I saw her I knew she was in trouble long before she tried to crawl into the casket. She held it together, though, when it counted. Giving me a big hug when she saw me was a huge relief at a time when I really needed it. Looking around that room, though, was tonic for me when I saw her doctors all standing tall in support of a family that they had worked with for years. Bobby Garrison and Tony Thomas had known the family for years, knew what was being said and circulated, and it didn't matter to them. They were compassionate men of ideal and principle, and I was proud to be in their company.

In spite of all that grief that day, I tried to look on the positive side. I believe that in the hereafter I will meet every person, I have taken care of that has gone before me, and that they will know by seeing into my heart that without exception, I always did my very best for them--anything less would not be right for them or for me. So for me guilt and suspicion had to give a way to faith and hope. I knew that in the sweet bye-and-bye Cyndy was talking up a storm, running all over the place without falling, and having the time of her afterlife.

"Have I not commanded you? Be strong and courageous. Do not be frightened, and do not be dismayed, for the Lord your God is with you wherever you go." - Joshua 1:9

Therefore I knew she was just fine but she had a family that was not.

God is not done with His work in our families or us—not by a long shot, and then when Christ has finished the work on us, we will be one of the finest pieces of art He has created. At Cyndy's funeral we were in the eye of the storm. Although our grief and rage were far from being over, we were allowed a moment of grace to hear words of truth and know that the Lord was with us. We knew hope was on the horizon. Family members and friends encouraged us with stories about how Cyndy changed their lives. My big brother Jimmy remembered:

"In October of 1985, my kid sister Anne gave birth to a baby girl. Cyndy was very badly handicapped mentally and physically but she was still a beautiful creation of God. My family and I would see Cyndy only a few times a year usually at special events and holidays. I saw the struggles that were threatening to break down this unit, but God kept them together. They were determined to keep things as normal as possible, despite their growing family and their children's special needs. Cyndy did not communicate verbally; she seemed always to be quiet and introspective. My family is typically loud but no matter how loud we got, Cyndy was quiet. That quiet spirit really stood out to us. We noticed that nothing seemed to upset her.

In retrospect, I can see that Cyndy was a gift from God to our family. This small quiet life had accomplished something remarkable. She lived and loved without a word said in anger. Such is the Kingdom of Heaven, and this quiet life now sings to the glory of God forever!"

As Jesus said, in Matthew 19:14, 'Let the little children come to me and do not hinder them, for to such belongs the kingdom of heaven.'"

Our neighbor Monica Eaker who met Cyndy in April 1988 recalled:

"Cyndy had the prettiest eyes and sweetest smile. She never seemed to give anyone much trouble, and she always had a hug for me. I loved how observant she was. Cyndy would treat a simple thing like a block or ball as a treasure. Her little hands would turn it over repeatedly while her fingers felt the entire area. While outside she would look up at the sky or pick a leaf off a bush. Nothing escaped her pretty eyes or curious mind. No matter how sick she was Cyndy's spirit stayed strong. Even confined to a wheelchair, she always smiled and clapped her hands when she was happy. Nothing seemed to deter her from enjoying life. Even though I have many memories of Cyndy, these are the ones that make her such a special child to me.

Anyone who knew Cyndy learned such valuable lessons from her. Our lives become more meaningful when we take time to observe in detail the beautiful things God has shared with us. God made us to love other people and we receive a beautiful blessing when we do. God can truly sustain us in times of trouble so that ultimately we can enjoy life and let God's love shine through us. Many people could live for 80 years and not learn these truths. Cyndy knew them at a young age and I am so thankful that Cyndy was able to share them with me."

Cyndy let her light shine bright; she didn't hide it under a bushel or basket. Jesus says in Matthew 5:14-16,

'You are the light of the world. A city set on a hill cannot be hidden. Nor do people light a lamp and put it under a basket, but on a stand, and it gives light to all in the house. In the same way, let your light shine before others, so that they may see your good works and give glory to your Father who is in heaven.'

Cyndy did just that.

Our pastor Mark Bender and his wife Marlene have fond memories of Cyndy:

"Cyndy had no prejudices towards others. I remember how she would approach people with warm hugs and cheerful smiles. I recall one occasion in the nursery when she came and sat on my lap. She had a way of making everyone feel special. She displayed for us the love of our Savior who lovingly welcomed all into His presence.

I recall the courage and persevering nature Cyndy possessed in the midst of much trial and suffering. Despite her seizures, her stays in the hospital, and her bouts with sickness, she fought back with a tenacity that few people possess on this earth. I remember one occasion while in the hospital when Cyndy's dad told the nurses to make sure she was restrained better or she would get out of bed. They did not listen and, sure enough, Cyndy climbed out of bed. It was difficult to keep her down because she had a fighting spirit.

Cyndy was always busy doing something and loved to include others in her activities. I often wished that I had as much energy as Cyndy. She was full of life and vigor. It was contagious for all of us to learn how to love life in the same way as Cyndy."

Dr. White reflected on Cyndy's death and life:

"When you think about it, there is probably a Cyndy in every family, if you look back far enough in time. Every life, long and short, touches many others but Cyndy—she was special. She disproved the naysayers, taught myself and her other doctors some things, and reminded all of us that happiness is not an absolute but depends on your frame of reference. To paraphrase my grandfather, she got a great ride for her nickel. So play long and play hard, my angel.

Cyndy had her disabilities but she had her way of brightening peoples' lives with her smiles and hugs. She was used by God to bring glory and honor to Himself, as describe in John 9:1-5

"...as he passed by, he saw a man blind from birth. And his disciples asked him, 'Rabbi, who sinned, this man, or his parents, that he was born blind?' Jesus answered, 'It was not that this man sinned, or his parents, but that the works of God might be displayed in him. We must work the works of him who sent me while it is day; night is coming, when no one can work. As long as I am in the world, I am the light of the world.'"

Mark's mother, Cyndy's grandmother Harrell, remembers:

"Our Cyndy was a very loving baby, whose love seemed to grow with each passing day. She had her 'good' days, and she had her 'just not so good' days. We never heard a complaint or as much as whine when she had a rough day. She was always happy and made us all laugh at some of her antics. She brought out the best in people and taught us what innocence, purity, love, and trust meant. I know Mark and Anne had their hands full, but they never complained.

I remember when she was very young and we put her in her play-pen. She would reach up to us and give us sweet wet kisses and hugs. One time when Bill and I went to have dinner with Mark, Anne, and the kids I sat on the sofa to read to them. Cyndy climbed on my lap, nuzzled my neck, curled up, and went to sleep while I finished the story. She was so precious, and I always felt that a little bit of heaven had been born in her. One day, we will see our sweet Cyndy jumping, running, walking, and what a nice time we will have then! What a rich blessing our Cyndy was to all who knew her and us...THANK YOU, GOD!"

Another friend from church, Wanda Rawls, called Cyndy:

"...a rose who never got to completely bloom. She is in total splendor now in heaven--healthy and full of peace and joy. Cyndy showed me how much God loves each of us, regardless of our abilities, beauty, or health. He showed me this by how much Mark and Anne loved Cyndy simply because she was their child. We do not have to be beautiful, gifted, or healthy for God to love us. He takes us as we are imperfections and all. What a relief to know the Creator loves us simply because we are His. The unconditional love Mark and Anne had for Cyndy is a perfect example of our Father's love for each of us."

Cyndy understood His love. Even though some people shunned her because of her handicaps Cyndy did not let them bother her; she knew she was God's special child and that she would be in heaven when her time came. I think of the Beatitudes in Matthew 5:3-12 when I think of Cyndy:

"Blessed are the poor in spirit, for theirs is the kingdom of heaven. Blessed are those who mourn, for they shall be comforted. Blessed are the meek, for they shall inherit the earth. Blessed are those who hunger *and thirst for righteousness, for they shall be satisfied. Blessed are the merciful, for they shall receive mercy. Blessed are the pure in heart, for they shall see God. Blessed are the peacemakers, for they shall be called sons of God. Blessed are those who are persecuted for righteousness' sake, for theirs is the kingdom of heaven. Blessed are you when others revile you and persecute you and utter all kinds of evil against you falsely on my account. Rejoice and be glad, for your reward is great in heaven, for so they persecuted the prophets who were before you."*

I think that when Jesus comes back and gathers His children together in heaven, I will be surprised at how many people are lined up to see Cyndy—just to see how she's doing and to thank her. To think that God used my little girl who was so weak and small in the world's eyes to show others His love! God did not make a mistake in making Cyndy; He knew exactly what He was doing even when I doubted Him. That fact always brings me great comfort.

Prayer:
Thank you, Lord, for showing us that things happen in Your time and not ours, and that we are all a part of Your perfect plan. Thanks for showing us how fragile life is and that when our time here on earth is over, if we have accepted You as our Lord and Savior, we will return home to You.
In Christ,
Amen

CHAPTER THIRTEEN

It is I... Be Not Afraid

"*But immediately Jesus spoke to them, saying, "Take heart; it is I. Do not be afraid." - Matthew 14:27*

P arents never expect to bury their children. Our children are supposed to bury us when we get old, but NEVER should we have to bury our children. Nevertheless, even after something as traumatic as the death of a child, life has its way of going on, whether we feel ready for marching or not. The day after the funeral is when reality sets in. All the out-of-town company has left and the pain really hits home.

However as soon as Cyndy was put in her grave we had to forget about grieving the loss of our oldest daughter and quickly pull ourselves together to get our other five children back. We were served with papers on Friday, January 3, 1997 and had to be in court the following Monday to answer to charges of neglect. Unfortunately, my neglecting our house became the ultimate reason that social services had taken our children from us. As we looked over all the state's allegations against us the possibility of ever getting the children back seemed bleak. Mark and I were not sure how we were going to get through the court date or whether charges would be filed against us. All we could do was put our hands in the Lord's hands and lean on Him for strength. Every time we heard something about the status of our case we felt like we were being

Cyndy was always light to carry – no trouble at all.

put under a microscope and scrutinized.

> *DR. WHITE:* I first heard about social services removing the rest of the children from Dr. Garrison, Cyndy's pediatrician for years and a fantastic person. Obviously I was in disbelief. Child abuse and neglect are an unfortunate reality in today's world and I frequently see evidence of it literally every day. But here? This family? Once again all those scenarios of Cyndy's last night came rushing back, punctuated by the inquiries and questions from the social service investigators, which had to be tough and blunt. Did I know this? Was I aware of that?

At our court date Mark and I had to give evidence of our fitness to care for our children and answer any concerns about our health and mental status. It soon became apparent to me that the city expected me to be some kind of supermom, able to function normally with no sadness after we lost our daughter. I felt like the state expected us to forget about Cyndy and just focus on our other children. Social Services expected me to bounce back from Cyndy's death within a week. If I showed any signs of depression Social Services would deem it a reason to not return the children home.

We appeared in court with our family, friends, and doctors; our pastor, Mark Bender, appeared for extra support. Everything about the courtroom fueled tension and resentment on both sides. Some of the social workers were angry that our doctors were backing us up. Dr. Garrison testified on our behalf; he encouraged the court to give our children back to us stating that he had seen the children often and never noticed any kind of abuse.

The state wanted to know why both Doctors Garrison and White were so adamant about the state returning the children back to us given how our neglected our house looked. Neighbors, teachers, church members, counselors, family members all testified along with our doctors but none of it seemed to be making a difference. The state wanted to examine Cyndy's autopsy reports, which would take an additional six weeks, before it would make a decision about our children. Even though the initial autopsy reports stated that she died a natural death, the state wanted to wait for the final reports. In the meantime the children had to remain in foster care. We couldn't understand why the state wanted to claim that we had abused Cyndy but NEVER subpoenaed the medical examiner to testify about Cyndy's autopsy.

Early on the state wanted to place some of the blame of Cyndy's death on Dr. White since some of the medications he had prescribed for her were on the high side of normal.

DR. WHITE: An important fact in the state's case was that a blood level of Mogadon that I had obtained just days before Cyndy's death was ten to fifteen times the limit of normal, even four times higher than the high levels that we had recorded when we were pushing her doses up when she was younger. How could this be?

Obviously the coroner was involved and I fielded many inquiries from her as well. I was obviously hoping that no evidence of foul play would be found and that after rechecking postmortem blood levels and rechecking the blood tests in question the abnormally high level would be a mistake. Between phone calls and visits to the coroner, she sorted out that

Cyndy's blood levels were not too high and let me sit in on the brain examination; she even saved some cortex for me to brain bank for later, but in the rush of events I lost it. The weeks that it took to sort things out came excruciatingly slow with too little happening in between. Over the years I have been right sometimes and wrong sometimes; I am a doctor, not a profiler. This time, though, I was right.

Dr. White insisted that the lab repeat the test on the same blood draw to see if a mistake had been made; it had and the state could find no evidence of foul play. Although Mark and I knew that he was feeling just as hurt and angry as we were about Cyndy's death and the court case we didn't know everything he was going through. Several years would pass before we knew exactly how much Dr. White had suffered, and for that our hearts still ache.

Social Services alleged that our children had been physically abused and neglected but our doctors disagreed with their findings. They testified to what they knew was true even though their very careers were put in jeopardy for not backing the state's case. It was strange that social services didn't call the coroner. The medical examiner had called Dr. White and asked him to drop by the morgue and look at the size of Cyndy's brain. She wanted to know how Cyndy lived as long as she did with her brain being so small. The coroner questioned him about Cyndy's ability to walk and do things such as sitting up and or eating. She admitted that it was wonderful that Cyndy lived to be 11.

Dr. White had been telling me for years that Cyndy lived as long as she did because of the exceptional care and love she received from her family and doctors. Doctors Garrison and White affirmed us as parents; they knew we loved our children and did our best for them.

However the court still refused to rule in our favor. We knew we had an uphill battle ahead of us. We knew that the Lord was going to work in His timing and that nothing was going to stand in the way of the Lord. We were in His hands and He would shelter us from all wrong.

"Hear my cry, O God,
listen to my prayer;
from the end of the earth I call to you
when my heart is faint.
Lead me to the rock
that is higher than I,
for you have been my refuge,
a strong tower against the enemy." - Psalm 61:1-3

God was working for our good even through the difficult process of getting our children back. Mark and I underwent psychological evaluations and we discovered that both our therapist and our psychologist were Christians. However the person who administered the testing was not a Christian. When she made me interpret inkblots on cards and I said that all I could see in them were angels it made her angry! She told our therapist, Charles that I was "really spiritual," but I am not sure if she thought that was a good thing or not! It made Charles laugh though, and fight even harder for us when social services would call about supposed claims.

I started to believe that even though things seemed bleak, God was with me. He would never leave me alone or give me more than I could handle with His help. Mark and I knew that God was with us and that He would shield us from all evil. Our hope and trust was in God alone.

"Let us hold fast the confession of our hope without wavering, for
he who promised is faithful." - Hebrews 10:23

We received several monetary gifts over the next few days and weeks to help pay for our legal and medical costs. One monetary gift came from my friend Monica, who I knew did not have much. I was reminded of the story in the gospels of the widow's mite. Like the widow Monica cheerfully gave all she had out of her poverty. We are still friends to this day.

Christ promised that He would never leave or forsake us, and He did stay with us. The more I cried, the tighter He would hold me. God was using this enormously difficult time to draw me closer to Him. That in itself was worth the hardship. In spite of our weakness Christ was looking out for us and providing our needs. He had touched hearts of people we did not think He would use to help us.

Things were not all positive and easy during this time, though. I still missed Cyndy and struggled constantly with my grief. Occasionally, I would walk into the house, see Cyndy lying on the floor in front of the bathroom, blue, and still. I would go into screaming spells, knowing that her airway had collapsed, causing her death. Life was still very hard. God was with me, but it was still very hard. There were days I would cry all day long, from the time I woke up until I fell asleep. Throughout the day I would look for any and everything that had Cyndy's scent.

With no children in our house the month of January was very trying for us. I was used to Mark working and the children keeping me busy. The sound of silence was overwhelming. I didn't know what to do with all the time I had on my hands. I felt like I should have been doing something every minute. I was crying all day every day, and I did not know if I was going to make it through each passing day. I wanted all my children home again. Depression hit hard and nights were the worst. When Mark was working nights he couldn't take me with him. The house seemed so big and every little noise scared me. Monica would sit and talk with me many nights just to keep me from taking my own life. We would talk until the sun came up.

Social Services returned Mark Jr. and Richard to our home in February. They had been kept in a state psychiatric hospital and after 30 days no longer wanted to pay for their care. Because the state ordered that neither Dr. Garrison nor White could have contact with the boys while they were in foster care we had a hard time getting the boys medications back in order, yet they quickly ordered for us to "fix" the boys when they sent them home. The state hired a company to send workers to observe us day in and day out from the time the boys got home from school until they were in bed at night. How could we resume any kind of normal life with these strangers in our midst? They were eating all our food and always hovering over us. I felt trapped in my own house, with these people watching every move we made.

When they sent the older boys back home, we were expected to perfectly handle four handicapped children who had diagnoses from mild to severe degrees of disabilities despite our grief, the children's grief, and having no help or understanding from the state. None of the workers placed in our home had training on how to handle handicapped children. I knew more than they did on how to work with the boys. They would let the boys go off and tear apart my house, and then I was expected to clean it all up. Their presence just heightened my stress and anger, and I was crying all the time. When the boys would act out then the social workers yelled at me asking why I couldn't control them? I was their mom, and in their minds I should have been able to handle them no matter what.

Monica pleaded with me just to be patient, and said that if I needed to vent she was there for me. She heard me vent a lot. If the boys were not trashing the house, then I was dealing

No video games when I was little.

with suspicions that the staff was stealing medications from the boys because we did not have enough meds to get through the month. Meals became a battlefield because the workers' presence agitated the boys, which led to them acting up. I felt constantly on edge, and I would blow up every time they would do something wrong.

I just kept desperately crying out to God, "Please, help me out here!" I would ask God to make everything just go away. We were praying daily that God would just remove the company that social services had placed in our home. After about a month of living under this pressure our social worker started noticing that I was crying every time she called. Finally she decided to come out for a visit and find out what was happening. When she went to leave she called Mark and me outside to speak about the workers; they followed us out asking us to come in and stop the boys from fighting. This angered the social worker so much that she went back and fired the company the next morning. God had answered our prayers.

A few days after the social services removed the in-home service they placed a different in-home group with us from Institute for Family Centered Services. The workers Janet, Dale, Kathleen, Debbie, Ken, and a few others helped us out. They were a breath of fresh air. Our family grew closer together, my house stayed cleaner, and I was able to stay on top of things because these workers were not afraid to get their hands dirty and they really helped us with the boys.

During the time that we were grieving Cyndy's death, surviving the removal of our children, and then getting them back and battling with social services, our marriage was being tested as well. Mark and I were at a crucial place that could make or break our marriage. Dealing with Cyndy's death gave God the opportunity to work on Mark and me and to show us how to care for each other even in the midst of a horrible situation. God had put Mark and I exactly where He wanted us so that He could do awesome things in our relationship. We were not ready for what the Lord had in store for us. Mark and I were struggling to get along even before Cyndy died and we were really fighting to keep our marriage together. However, what looked on the outside like an evil situation—our family being split apart—became a blessing. Mark and I became closer during that month that the kids were gone. We had time to learn how to love each other all over again. Because we had been so busy going our own ways, we had forgotten who the other one was. God used that month to bring us closer together. Not only did Mark and I become closer to each other, but we also drew closer to God Himself. We went places together to learn more about each other; Mark even took me to work with him when he could so that I did not have to be alone at night when I was scared to be alone.

It was a miracle that God saved our marriage. It can be so easy for a husband and wife to pull away from each other in the middle of such pain. We did not deserve to have God intervene so graciously and hold us together. But he did have other things in mind for our family, and He was faithful to love us enough to save us from ourselves.

Prayer:
Lord, thank you for loving us when we are not lovable. Thank you for being with us and carrying us when our pain is unbearable. You said you will never leave us or forsake us, and we lean on that promise.
In Christ's name,
Amen

CHAPTER FOURTEEN

Our Sister Sees Jesus

"My comfort in my suffering is this: Your promise preserves my life." – Psalm 119:50

Cyndy's death had an enormous impact on our remaining five children. They wrestled with a myriad of emotions and questions. What exactly happened to Cyndy? Why are we not with our parents anymore? Why are we in this hospital? What did we do that was so bad to deserve being kept here? Where is our sister Cyndy? Will we ever see her again? Some of the questions had to remain unanswered: why did God let this happen to us? There was nothing the children did to be treated as they were. It was what Mark and I did not do that we should have done to keep the children more comfortable and put less stress on them. Yet if we look hard enough we can usually see that something good can come from every unpleasant situation. If we will learn from our mistakes a blessing will come about in due time.

As we welcomed the children back home and tried to recover as a family we saw how the children individually grieved Cyndy's death. Our oldest, Mark Jr., was 12 when Cyndy died. Since Mark is autistic, he struggles in expressing his feelings. Mark has always been particularly caring and sensitive so Cyndy's death was a blow to him. To this day when we mention Cyndy he will say that he misses his sister. We know

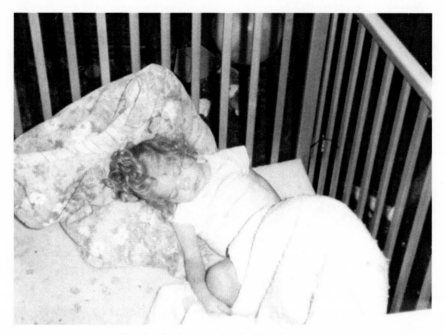

Sleeping Cyndy was an angel without her wings.

that he still thinks about Cyndy sometimes when he asks for her picture. Whenever we pass the cemetery where Cyndy is buried, Mark will point and say, "Cyndy is over there. Let's go see Cyndy." He will tell us that "Cyndy, Angel (our cat), and Granddaddy are over there." We cannot go over to Mark Sr.'s mom's house without going by the cemetery. Mark will tell us that Cyndy is in Heaven, "with God," and point to the sky.

Our second son Richard was nine at the time of Cyndy's death. Like Mark Jr., he is autistic and has difficulty articulating his feelings. He will come up to us unexpectedly and tell us that he misses Cyndy. Richard is determined to keep his sister's memory alive. He will remind us of Cyndy's birthday or point out things in the house that used to belong to Cyndy. He wants to take flowers to her grave often. It is almost as though he is afraid we will forget about her because she is gone. Richard will tell us about dreams of Cyndy which upset him because when he wakes up she is no longer here.

When Cyndy died our two youngest children, Buddy and Joel, were five and two years old respectively. Both boys are severely autistic. Buddy will tell you he remembers Cyndy and mainly repeat what the other children say about Cyndy. Joel does not talk but he will take Cyndy's picture off the wall and smile at it. If you take Cyndy's picture away from him Joel will start to cry. When Joel first came home from foster care he would not go in the bedroom that he shared with Cyndy and Katie. He would stand at the door of the room and cry.

On top of dealing with the loss of their sister our children had to deal with the trauma of being placed in foster care. Mark Jr., Richard, and Buddy were put into a psychiatric hospital. The entire world of familiarity and safety had collapsed. When they saw Cyndy unmoving on the floor they started to cry. They couldn't understand what was wrong with her or what was happening: people in the house taking pictures and fingerprinting, pointing their fingers, screaming, and yelling. We were supposed to be celebrating a holiday, but instead our family was in chaos.

When the boys were placed in the hospital, their behavior worsened and the psychiatrist didn't know their medication history. The anticipated "improvement" away from our "toxic" home didn't happen. After 30 days in the hospital, Buddy went to live in a foster home and the other two were sent home. We learned later that Buddy's foster mother started to make him call her "mom," which sickened me to no end. I am Buddy's mom. How could she do that to him or me?

When Mark Jr. and Richard came home they asked so many questions. They wanted to know where Cyndy was and why God took their sister. We had to remind them repeatedly that Cyndy was in heaven with God...that she was able to walk without falling down constantly and could even talk now. We also assured them that Cyndy would no longer have seizures and she was not sick anymore. We tried to tell them everything was going to be just fine, yet we were not sure ourselves. All we could do was put our faith totally in God and God only.

Katie is our only non-disabled child. She was only six when Cyndy died and she was placed in a foster home. Katie was returned home to us in March, approximately a month after Mark Jr. and Richard came home. She had problems getting along with her foster father. During the time she was in foster care Katie ran away from the home. Since our house was right by her school Katie would evade her teachers and run home from school too. In some ways this whole ordeal has been hardest on Katie since she is fully aware of everything that happened. Katie recalls how she felt when Cyndy died and when she was taken out of our home.

"I will never forget the morning my sister died. I woke up all excited about New Year's Day parade on TV. As I wiped my eyes and climbed out of bed I noticed that Cyndy was still asleep...at least I thought she was. I was slowly trying to tiptoe past Cyndy so that I would not wake her up. When I got out of the room I went racing down the stairs. I heard my Dad getting my brothers' and sister's medicines out and starting to give the morning meds. I was excited because Dad would let me give Cyndy her meds since she took her meds so easily. I felt like a real doctor or nurse being able to give my big sister her meds. I went running up the stairs to give her the meds....at least I thought I was going to give Cyndy her meds.

As I walked into the room I saw that my sister was still asleep. I wanted her to wake up but she just wasn't waking up; something about when I touched her wasn't right. I remember how cold she felt when I touched her. I called out her name trying to wake her up. I remember how bluish-purplish her face was but I didn't think anything about it at first. I kept shaking Cyndy to wake her up. I got angry that she wouldn't respond so I reached over to pull her hair. To this day I feel bad about pulling Cyndy's hair to wake her up.

I finally gave up and went back down stairs with her meds; I told my Dad 'Cyndy won't wake up.' My Dad was busy but he said, 'Alright, just wait and I will give them to her in a minute.'

About five minutes later, Daddy came upstairs with me to wake up Cyndy. He walked in the room, calling out Cyndy's name and then took her by the arm to turn her over. He got a surprised nervous look on his face when he turned Cyndy over; I knew something alarming must have happened because he dropped the medicine. I was wondering why Dad did that when he shouted to my mom 'Honey she's gone! She's gone!'

My mom yelled up to my Dad, 'What do you mean 'she's gone?' Running up the stairs as fast as my Mom's legs would carry her, she was screaming, 'No, she's not gone!' She came running upstairs so fast that it scared me to death. She was demanding to know where Cyndy had gone. Then she picked up my sister's lifeless body and ran with her downstairs to do CPR on her, hopefully to wake her up.... My dad followed quickly behind my mom, yelling at my brothers and me to stay in our rooms. I went into my brothers' room instead because we were not sure what was happening but knew it had to do with Cyndy. The looks on my parents faces was like they had heard a scary story. I had never seen my parents so upset. While I was in the room I kept hearing my Mom and Dad screaming at the top of their lungs---I wondered what they meant about her being dead. There was no way my sister could be dead could she? Is Cyndy ever going to wake up? Please Cyndy wake up do not be what my parents think... you cannot be dead. Oh, please do not be whatever being dead meant... Why are my parents walking around all upset? Cyndy you are going to be okay? Oh PLEASE Be.

I kept praying that Cyndy was just seizuring and that maybe she needed the doctor's help to stop the seizure...I was not ready to accept that my sister was dead.

The next thing I remember was hearing sirens coming from all directions. The house was filling up with the paramedics, police... they were coming through the house...taking pictures...more police were coming and they were going in all the rooms and dusting for fingerprints. I wondered what did the police have to do with Cyndy seizuring? Why were they asking so many questions about my parents? If Cyndy was just having seizures why were they taking pictures and dusting for fingerprints? My mom was screaming and would not stop.

Soon Marge, a very sweet woman from our church, came to watch us children while the police were questioning my parents. I kept wondering why the police would not let my parents be together--- my Mom and Dad needed each other. Didn't the police understand? My parents did not do anything to cause my sister's death...why were they being so uncaring? I thought this nightmare would never end. My mom's sister Mary came and ended up in the middle of the mess that kept getting bigger. When she realized that we had not yet eaten she went and got us some chicken from Hardees. The next thing I knew my aunt was screaming that she was going to take us kids with her and that they were not going to take us kids away... at the time I wondered what she meant by that—what is happening that now my Aunt Mary was here screaming and yelling at the police? Why was she saying that she was taking us kids home with her and not them---what was the meaning of that? Who was trying to take us?

We were ushered out of the house without being allowed to tell our parents goodbye. We could not hug our parents, even speak with to them, or tell them bye. As I looked for my parents I was screaming and kicking and even biting the social workers. As I looked around I saw that Cyndy's lifeless body was on the floor covered by a sheet. All of us children were put in separate cars. I remember my parents begging them please put my baby brother Joel in the same home with me. I wondered where we were going and when were we coming back home.

The social worker told me that they were just getting a babysitter for my parents since my sister had died and my parents needed some help to get through the death and planning for the funeral, but they would be back for me later that evening to take me home. I wanted so much to go to my sister's funeral, but no one came for me and I kept asking when I could go home. Hours turned into days and weeks into months. When I saw my parents I begged them to clean up the house so I could come home. I wanted to go home so badly, and I began to wonder what I did that was so bad that my parents did not love me anymore.

I had fun running away from the home where I was staying. My teacher would run after me and not catch me until I was at my parents' house. My parents were not home for me to see them. I remember one day after Richard and Mark were home my mom was at the school to check on Richard and I saw my mom. We were able to touch only through the glass window in the office. The only reason I was able to do that was the teacher saw my mom in the office and called me back to see her. My first grade teacher was so nice. She was very helpful and understanding.

Seeing my parents was hard on me since I always wanted to go home. I would cry and tell the social worker who would come get me from school to tell my parents that I wanted to go home. I would beg her every time. One time after it had snowed I told my parents how my foster father put snow down my pants. Another time when I was sick my foster parents made me sleep in the bathroom. One thing I liked was I had a foster sister that was the same age as me, but she would always get me into trouble. I was not sure she liked me since she was the only child in that family and had everything she wanted. Later on she and I were in the same classes and we became good friends.

After my parents and doctors complained about my foster parents pushing to either remove me from their home or send me back home I told the social worker where I wanted to go. Two days before I went home, I saw an angel that looked like Cyndy. I really thought she was Cyndy and that she had came back from the dead. She was so beautiful and radiant. Cyndy told me that I would be going home very soon. Hearing my sister speak blessed my soul, yet made me sorrowful that she had to leave. I begged the angel - Cyndy - not to leave when she appeared to me. The next morning I told my foster mother that I was going home. She told me that she knew nothing about me going home and that I should stop asking. That evening my foster mother told me that I was going home the next day. I was so excited!

When I got home, I told my parents about seeing Cyndy. They told me that I really did not see Cyndy, but an angel. I really felt blessed

Our children remember their sister.

that I had seen her. My parents told me that about how in Hebrews 13:2 it says that sometimes we will see angels and even entertain them unaware.

Cyndy died when I was in the first grade. As I walked down the aisle graduating from high school I could feel my sister's sprit with me. I knew that Cyndy was wishing me well. If only she could have been with me bodily I would have been happy. I miss my sister a great deal and wish she were back here with us. Yet I am thankful and relieved that she is well now and not suffering anymore. I will keep living for the Lord and wait patiently to see her again, either when the Lord comes again or when my time comes."

Prayer:

Thank you, Lord, for watching over us and keeping us safe. Thank you for sending your angels, as in Psalm 91:11-12: "For he will command his angels concerning you to guard you in all your ways. On their hands they will bear you up, lest you strike your foot against a stone." Thank you Lord for being here in our time of trouble. Thank you for tucking us under your mighty wings of love.

In Christ,

Amen

CHAPTER FIFTEEN

Even God Was Angry When Jesus Died

"And behold, the curtain of the temple was torn in two, from top to bottom. And the earth shook, and the rocks were split. The tombs also were opened. And many bodies of the saints who had fallen asleep were raised, and coming out of the tombs after his resurrection, they went into the holy city and appeared too many. When the centurion and those who were with him, keeping watch over Jesus, saw the earthquake and what took place, they were filled with awe and said, 'Truly this was the Son of God!'" - Matthew 27:51-54

The grief and pain that a parent endures after losing a child evolves over time. It can be a period of months or even years before the hurt subsides to the point of being tolerable. Recuperating happens in stages. When Cyndy died I was riddled with shock, anger, numbness, disbelief, and sadness. I just wanted to die. I was unable to sleep or eat for periods of time and I cried constantly. Nobody could reach me or help me when I would just completely shut down. There was a tremendous void in our lives without Cyndy and my home life felt meaningless without her. Yet one day I came to my senses and realized that if we wanted to heal from Cyndy's death we needed to draw near to God. Without God, we CANNOT HEAL...ONLY GOD CAN GIVE US HEALING IN OUR SOULS!

I learned that there are five stages to grief - shock and denial, anger, bargaining, depression, and acceptance - and everyone cycles through them in different ways and at different times.

Shock and Denial

When Mark called down to me and told me that Cyndy was gone I did not want to believe that Cyndy could possibly be dead. I was in the first stage of grief – shock and denial. Grieving parents can stay in that stage for a couple of months or longer. Mark and I were able to deny Cyndy's death at first because we did not see her remains until the day before her funeral. Almost three days passed before we were forced to confront Cyndy's death. The day before Cyndy's funeral, when we saw her in the casket there was no denying that Cyndy had died but the biggest slap in the face - when we felt like we had been run over by a bulldozer - was the hour of the funeral. After the funeral the realization set in that we would not see her again until we enter eternity.

When I was in denial I wanted to find a valid reason for Cyndy's death. I did not want to accept the truth, which was that Cyndy's airway had collapsed. I couldn't accept that as a reason because the thought that she suffered was incomprehensible. I know that God knows the day and time to the second that He will take us home to Him, but I could not accept that was Cyndy's time.

Maybe I was an inadequate parent, or maybe God was just being mean to me. I kept asking God, "Why did it have to be Cyndy? Why couldn't it have been me?" I just couldn't handle my thoughts and questions. Of course now as I look back I can see how God was working in our lives. God sent us through the furnace to sharpen our faith in Christ. Our sorrow was intended to strengthen our faith in God and to trust Him instead of depending on ourselves.

Anger

When Cyndy died I put a lot of blame on my husband Mark, thinking that Cyndy would still be alive if he had left her downstairs that New Year's Eve. I blamed my son Joel that he may have lain on Cyndy and caused her to die. I blamed myself for not being a good mother to Cyndy. I felt upset with Dr. White for him even revealing to me that Cyndy was going to die. Even though he tried to break the news to me so gently and tactfully, I felt like his prognosis was a death sentence for Cyndy. I do know, however, that Dr. White was trying so fiercely not to offend me, nor add any more distress to my already-overwhelming problems or to hurt me anymore then he had to hurt me. But he had to be honest and tell me that my suspicions about Cyndy's condition were true. I knew by the expression on his face, that the truth hurt him as much as it hurt me.

Now, I did not and would not hold Dr. White responsible for Cyndy's death. Deep down, I knew he had done ALL he could possibly do. Cyndy was simply tired and ready to be with her Creator. Mark and I were very thankful that Dr. White and Dr. Garrison had given her such excellent care while she was on this earth. They were part of the reason that she lived as long as she did.

When Cyndy died I was too terrified to lay direct blame on God. I hid my anger against God deep within my heart. But my secret thoughts were spiteful toward Him. He could have kept Cyndy alive. He could have let me know something was going wrong in the early hours of the day of her death. I have even questioned Dr. White about why my "mommy radar" didn't go off that night. He said that night my radar was silenced because God had better plans for Cyndy. If only He would have let my daughter live. It was only a matter of time before all these painful thoughts spilled out. With all the people I wanted to blame for losing Cyndy, I had to acknowledge that I was furious with God most of all and myself.

Not long after I started writing this book I read a book entitled *Sit Down God...I'm Angry* by R.F. Smith Jr. Reading that book I realized that I was not alone in my anger toward God. The book reflected my own feelings of distress and pain. I found it very hard to pray to God and really, I did not want to hear what He had to say. I learned that these are all normal feelings.

I also noticed in this book the author talked about wanting to make contact with his son beyond the grave, and that he looked for ways to be in communication with his son after his death. When Cyndy died I, too, wanted to make contact with her so badly that I did not care what it did to my family or anyone around me. I did not care that I spent thousands of dollars on people who had ungodly motives...people who promised me I could find out more about Cyndy. God bless R.F. Smith, Jr. for showing me the right way to deal with my anger toward God and the other people that hurt me in the process of losing Cyndy. It was a huge relief to realize that I was normal and not going crazy! Yet, I also realized that trying to get in touch with Cyndy didn't please God one bit.

Neither did it please my family nor did it set well with Dr. White. Pastor Mark did all he could to help me see that my deeds were not fitting for a Christian while gently setting me back on the path of righteousness.

As I read passages in the Bible I found that even our Heavenly Father was angry when His only begotten Son was killed. In the Bible, Matthew tells of the earthquake that the Lord caused over the death of His son.

> "And behold, the curtain of the temple was torn in two, from top to bottom. And the earth shook, and the rocks were split. The tombs also were opened. And many bodies of the saints who had fallen asleep were raised, and coming out of the tombs after his resurrection, they went into the holy city and appeared too many. When the centurion and those who were with him, keeping watch over Jesus, saw the earthquake and what took place, they were filled with awe and said, 'Truly this was the Son of God!'" - Matthew 27:51-54

God was angry over the loss of His Son. God knew the pain I felt over losing Cyndy long before I felt the pain. He cried with me over Cyndy's death. He knew the hurt and disappointment I felt and continue to feel to this day.

It has been 14 years since we lost Cyndy and I still find that I get angry over her being gone. I have read that a crucial part of healing is to forgive your loved one for dying. At times I would get angry with Cyndy since she lost her will to live back in August 1996, when she coded and had to be brought back to life. Cyndy just seemed to have had no desire to stay alive any longer. Mark and I believe she had a glimpse of heaven and longed to be there where there is no sickness or pain. In the book of Revelation, John tells us what Heaven will be like.

> "He will wipe away every tear from their eyes, and death shall be no more, neither shall there be mourning nor crying nor pain anymore, for the former things have passed away...For the Lamb in the midst of the throne will be their shepherd, And he will guide them to springs of living water, and God will wipe away every tear from their eyes...Then the angel showed me the river of the water of life, bright as crystal, flowing from the throne of God and of the Lamb." - Rev. 21:4, 17; 22:1

Knowing this, I could not blame Cyndy for wanting to be there. I just wish that I could be with her there myself at this very moment. I think about Cyndy at least a dozen times a day. I wish I could just hug and hold her once more. I know I will have all eternity to be with her in

Heaven but I just long to see her right now.

My grief for Cyndy changes over time. In December just shy of the ten-year mark of her death I sank into a deep depression. I had gotten to the point that I really missed Cyndy and wanted so much to be in Heaven with her. I even tried to take my life. Yes, I know that taking my life in my own hands IS WRONG. Now I have grieved to the point that I can freely say that I was furious with God for taking my daughter from me. He had the authority to keep her alive to this day. Yes, I would have been much happier if she was still here. But would I have understood the profound meaning of the love of Christ and His peace that passes understanding if she were still here today? God took away my daughter to give me something better—a greater dependence on Him and a fuller realization of His incredible love for me. What more could I ask of Him? One book that also helped me was *Will I Ever Be Whole Again?* by Sandra Aldrich. Sandra helped me see that I can go on and she showed me the steps to becoming whole again.

Bargaining

Usually when a loved one is expected to die, we begin to plead with God, promising to do something in exchange for his or her life to be spared. For example before Dad's surgery for colon cancer I promised God that I would be a better person, pray, read the Bible or whatever He wanted if only He would let Dad pull through. Several times he came close to death but recovered. We pleaded with God up until the day Dad finally died.

The same with Cyndy - when Dr. White told me Cyndy's life was winding down, I kept pleading with him to change Cyndy's meds and try something different to keep her from dying. Nothing else could be done – all of our options were over and things were no better. What was to be would be.

Depression

The depression stage is also known as the mourning stage. When Cyndy died, I didn't want to eat; Mark and my parents had to force food down me because I wasn't hungry. I had no energy to even get out of the bed. All I could do was cry. I just wanted to sleep or take an overdose and die. My house was a mess but I didn't care about anything during that time; grieving people typically don't care what others are saying about them while they are depressed. Some grieving people drink alcohol or do drugs to try and deaden the emotional pain. A certain amount

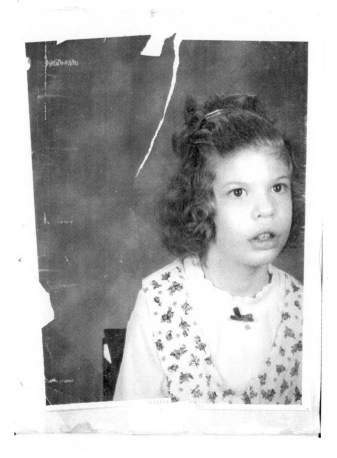

of depression is expected when a loved one dies but when it lasts for more than a month without any progress it's time to see a doctor or go to a support group and get help to deal with the death.

I often thought that because I couldn't keep my house orderly that I was an inadequate parent – perhaps that's why God took Cyndy. Or maybe God was just being mean because I wasn't thankful for years that I did have with her. I kept asking God, "Why did it have to be Cyndy? Why couldn't it have been me?"

Several different, horrifying ways of how Cyndy could have died plagued me at nighttime. It got so bad that I hated laying my head down on the pillow because I knew what awaited me. The scenes were so vivid that I would wake up in a cold sweat, screaming. I realized that those dreams were just fears I had of her dying in a way that I could have stopped.

I had so many questions after Cyndy died. How did she look in heaven in her glorified body? Could we have prevented her death from happening? Dr. Garrison and Dr. White were very polite and answered all of my questions, trying their best to explain what had happened to her. They reiterated that Cyndy had died quietly in her sleep. She simply had a final seizure, closed her eyes, and woke up in heaven. Dr. White repeated that Cyndy did not feel anything and that the seizure was probably not an extremely long one.

In my depression I began to obsess over wanting to see Cyndy in the casket. I went so far as to beg my friend Sam who is a funeral director to move Cyndy's body to another cemetery. He said he would but that it would be difficult to get permission and that it would be very expensive. He encouraged me to forget about the idea since her body was in no danger. Even if he did move her he was not going to let me see her remains. He kept reminding me that Cyndy's grave contained merely a shell; the real Cyndy was in heaven with God. With his encouragement and gentle truth from other family members and friends I finally moved to the next stage - accepting that Cyndy was gone.

Acceptance

Finally we come to a point where we can deal with our child's death and find that there is a way to move on in life. Life as we knew it will never be the same but it doesn't mean we've forgotten them.

Part of acceptance is coming to understand the reason for our child's death. I had to acknowledge that God knows the day and time - to the very second! - that He will take us home to Him. Certain things will affect our ability to accept our loss. For example, for me I didn't want a family portrait made after Cyndy's death because she was missing. Cyndy had been dead for 18 months before I agreed to have the picture made and I insisted that one of us hold a picture of her in it. After the first year things got a little better. Holidays and her birthday are still very hard for us. I still have depression around her birthday and the winter holidays until after the date of her funeral.

We still go to the cemetery to talk with Cyndy and put flowers on her grave. Our whole family likes keeping her grave adorned with flowers all year. Even though the death is still fresh in our minds we trust Christ to help us get through one day at a time. We know that we will see Cyndy again one day in the future, and that it will be a wonderful day.

"Blessed be the God and Father of our Lord Jesus Christ, the Father of mercies and God of all comfort, who comforts us in our entire affliction, so that we may be able to comfort those who are in any affliction, with the comfort with which we ourselves are comforted by God. For as we share abundantly in Christ's sufferings, so through Christ we share abundantly in comfort too. If we are afflicted, it is for your comfort and salvation; and if we are comforted, it is for your comfort, which you experience when you patiently endure the same sufferings that we suffer. Our hope for you is unshaken, for we know that as you share in our sufferings, you will also share in our comfort. For we do not want you to be ignorant, brothers, of the affliction we experienced in Asia. For we were so utterly burdened beyond our strength that we despaired of life itself. Indeed, we felt that we had received the sentence of death. But that was to make us rely not on ourselves but on God who raises the dead. He delivered us from such a deadly peril, and he will deliver us. On him, we have set our hope that he will deliver us again. You also must help us by prayer, so that many will give thanks on our behalf for the blessing granted us through the prayers of many." - 2 Cor. 1:3-11

God molds and strengthens our faith through our sorrow and He calls us to comfort others who are hurting through similar experiences. We are instruments of His healing as we build up Christ's body and glorify our Savior. God speaks His words of comfort in Isaiah:

"I, I am he who comforts you; who are you that you are afraid of man who dies, of the son of man who is made like grass...As one whom his mother comforts, so I will comfort you; you shall be comforted in Jerusalem."- Isaiah 51:12, 66:13

Christ stands beside me and comforts me—this truth is what keeps me going. We hope expectantly for that day when we will see Christ face to face and we will see our Cyndy again. We will be with her—and with God—forever. (Sandra is sending you hugs across the miles.)

Prayer:
Lord, thank You for the love You have for us. Teach us how to heal by putting our hands and faith in You. Teach us how to comfort others in our midst's that are hurting. May Your grace be rich and strong upon us.
In Christ's name,
Amen

CHAPTER SIXTEEN

Our Faith and Strength Is Built On Christ Alone

"Finally, brothers, whatever is true, whatever is honorable, whatever is just, whatever is pure, whatever is lovely, whatever is commendable, if there is any excellence, if there is anything worthy of praise, think about these things. What you have learned and received and heard and seen in me—practice these things, and the God of peace will be with you.

I rejoiced in the Lord greatly that now at length you have revived your concern for me. You were indeed concerned for me, but you had no opportunity. Not that I am speaking of being in need, for I have learned in whatever situation I am to be content. I know how to be brought low, and I know how to abound. In any and every circumstance, I have learned the secret of facing plenty and hunger, abundance and need. I can do all things through him who strengthens me." - Philippians 4:8-13

A year had come and gone since Cyndy's death. Four seasons later we thought that we were going to be able to deal with Cyndy being gone. It was time to move forward in our lives. Mark and I had no reason to anticipate that just a few days before our anniversary in April 1998 he would be in the ER with severe chest pain. He was kept overnight for tests and monitoring. The tests came back as normal and sent Mark home. I was somewhat relieved that maybe it was not Mark's heart but something nagged at me. Without a medical degree I couldn't argue with the doctors. They said Mark had an infection of the breastbone and that he had developed asthma.

On April 23, 1998, Mark woke up around midnight complaining of severe chest pain. He was sick to his stomach, sweating profusely, and having trouble breathing —classic symptoms of a heart attack. The female doctor in our primary doctor's practice said it could not be his heart, since he just recently had those tests in the ER. She kept saying that pain was normal for the infection of the breastbone, although it seemed anything but normal to me. I suspected a heart attack but the doctor insisted that Mark's tests had all been normal. Not trusting her advice I called the paramedics and they concurred with the doctor's diagnosis. The paramedics told us if Mark went to see the doctor again and tests came back saying it was an infection and not a heart attack, it would not be covered by our insurance. Mark did not want to go back to the hospital, so we stayed home.

We finally went to bed and all I could do was pray that God would just protect my husband. I prayed that I was wrong – that Mark had not had a heart attack. I was terrified that I would wake up in the morning and find my husband of 15 years dead just a year after our daughter's death. I just couldn't think of going on without my husband so soon after losing Cyndy. Once again I began to wonder why God was being so uncaring to me. It seemed like God was taking away anyone who meant something to me. I became so anxious I just wanted to die to keep from going through the pain of losing another family member so soon.

Mark returned to work after about six weeks of sick leave even though he really was not feeling physically up to returning to work. However we had bills piling up. Mark started working as much as he could to help us catch up financially. Neither one of us wanted to know if he had suffered a heart attack. We both stuck our heads in the sand and denied all the possibilities. We just prayed that our family could go back to being normal.

When Mark went back to work he chose to work nights, partly to avoid some of the breathing problems he was experiencing in the evenings when he tried to sleep. Mark tried his best to hide from me that he was not okay. He did not want me to know that his heart was the problem even if the test were negative. Mark thought if he denied that something serious was happening to him the crises would simply disappear. Mark's symptoms meant his heart was steadily getting worst. Mark worked night and day for two weeks straight until his health had gotten so bad that he could not keep going. I had already noticed the

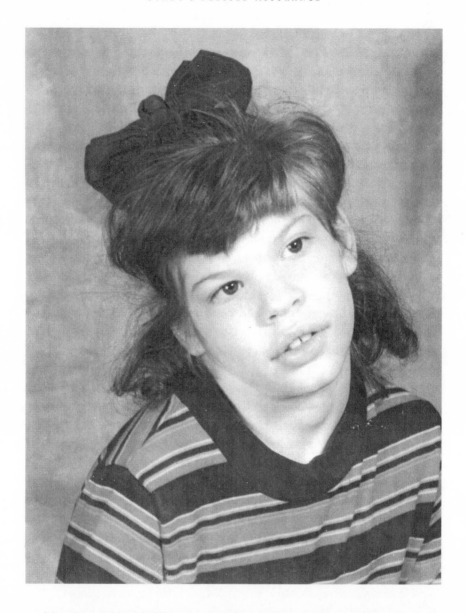

problems myself yet at first I wanted to ignore the signs and symptoms that Mark's health was rapidly declining. I knew something needed to be done quickly but how was I going to drag him to the hospital without him getting upset with me?

Mark had worked all night before Father's Day 1998. The children and I picked him up in the morning and we took him out for breakfast. Mark was due back at work that evening to work on another ship that was coming into port. The job would have meant working all night and until noon the next day. I told Mark and the hiring clerk that he had worked day and night for the last two weeks and that Father's Day was ours to be with him.

After coming home from breakfast Mark was resting on the sofa, and I noticed that his face was turning blue. I was concerned that his heart was not pumping efficiently. My God-given intuition (the one all moms have!) told me it wasn't asthma. When I called the insurance company the nurse told me Mark's symptoms were normal for someone diagnosed with asthma yet I knew that could not be right. With my emergency medical training and personal experience with asthma, I knew something was critically wrong. I had to run to the drug store to pick up some medicines and when I mentioned Mark's problems to the pharmacist he told me it sounded like heart problems.

I rushed home and talked Mark into going to the hospital. When the nurses did the EKG I realized that his heart was fluttering. It was the worst EKG reading I have ever seen, short of a flat line. The nurse tried to assure me that it was not his heart that was acting up, it was the machine. When she did the EKG the second time she ran out for a doctor. I knew Mark was critical when she returned with several doctors and nurses who began working on him furiously. The worst possible thoughts went through my mind. What would I do if, God forbid, He decided to take Mark home or if I had to make critical decisions because he had to go through open heart surgery?

Our worst nightmare had happened. Mark was in heart failure; his heart was on the verge of giving out. The doctor told me that had I gotten Mark to the hospital just 15 minutes later he would have died. He had suffered a massive heart attack and gone into heart failure. The doctor would not promise me that Mark was going to pull through but said he could tell me better in the next 72 hours.

Our world had been turned upside down once again. We weren't sure what was going to happen in the next hour much less the next couple of days. I feared Mark dying sometime during the night when I was not there. Why God are you doing this to my family...do not you know that we have five young children at home that need their daddy? Why God why? How are we going to make ends meet? We were already going under with our house payments, car payments, and other bills... how were we going to pull through?

Our family and church family helped us through the scariest days. The Lord heard my cries and provided for us even when my life was topsy turvy and I didn't know what to do. I had to put my hand into the Lord's hand once again and let Him walk me through another dark valley.

Two days after Mark was admitted to the hospital, the doctor did a heart catheterization, which showed massive, irreparable damage. There was no chance of doing bypass surgery since the heart muscle was dead behind the blockages. I went numb all over as I wondered how to tell Mark that he could die soon. I contemplated what would happen to my family, and how long it would take Mark to recover to where he could work again. To make matters more difficult Mark was in complete denial, telling family members either that he did not have a heart attack or that he had a minor infection that could be healed. Our in-home worker Janet Holden told family members that Mark had actually suffered a serious heart attack. Janet helped me to deal with the pain of his possible death and she helped me to remain optimistic about Mark's chances of recovery.

I struggled with anger – why weren't his heart attack symptoms caught and treated two months earlier? The doctors could have done something to stop further damage from being done.

Mark began to worry about how he was going to take care of his family after the doctors told him that he was finished working on the waterfront; he was going to have to stay home and rest. The guilt and burden of not being able to provide for his small children left Mark in agony. When I filed Mark's papers for sick pay and he saw what his compensation would be he felt a little better about not being able to work. Mark's retirement package provided us with a lump sum payout that enabled us to make some much-needed changes to the house.

We were on edge all the time, feeling the way we did when we were in constant crises mode with Cyndy. We worried every time Mark had chest pains. The doctor's prognoses indicated that Mark could probably live up to three years without a heart transplant but that a transplant was critical to ensuring Mark's full recovery or close to being normal as possible. He would not live more than a few years without a transplant. As I write this, it has been 10 years and counting since that first heart attack and Mark still has not needed a transplant. The Lord has been very good to us.

We have endured these 10 years through prayer and thanksgiving to our Heavenly Father for not taking Mark from us. We have learned to trust Christ in our darkest moments. When the doctors told us it was impossible for Mark live without a transplant, I recalled Luke 1:37, which says,

> "For nothing will be impossible with God." We have had to learn to cast "all your anxieties on him, because He cares for you." (1Peter 5:7). We also remembered in Psalm 91:11 where the psalmist writes, "For He will command his angels concerning you to guard you in all your ways."

The Bible assures us that God is watching over us in everything that we do, and He does care about our deepest sorrows.

When Cyndy died and Mark had his heart attack we learned that Christ looks after the faint-hearted and weak. When we feel like we cannot go on Christ pulls us through in His faithfulness. One of the most inspiring and comforting passages for me is Isaiah 40: 28-31:

> "Have you not known? Have you not heard? The Lord is the everlasting God, the Creator of the ends of the earth. He does not faint or grow weary; His understanding is unsearchable. He gives power to the faint, and to him who has no might He increases strength. Even youths shall faint and be weary, and young men shall fall exhausted; but they who wait for the Lord shall renew their strength; they shall mount up with wings like eagles; they shall run and not be weary; they shall walk and not faint."

Almost two years after Cyndy died, Mark was medically retired. We were amazed at what God could do when we prayed for His provision. Mark was shocked when he got a call from the Social Security office telling him $50,000 was being deposited into his account within the next two weeks and another $20,000 would be deposited for our children's care. With the money we were receiving from Social Security Mark and I wanted a marker for Cyndy's gravesite in time for her birthday. A friend of mine, Sam Purviance, who had owned a funeral home in the county I was from, was able to get a marker for us. I had told Sam I just wanted a plain marker but he knew I had a thing for angels and surprised us with the angels in the bottom corners of Cyndy's marker and an inscription saying: "Resting in the arms of Christ." Those words seemed most appropriate for Cyndy's resting place. The marker really helped us find some closure; it was placed on her grave just days before her thirteenth birthday in October 1999.

Mark had another heart attack on April 1, 2004 and it was the beginning of another uphill battle. When I had called my family, Mark's family, and Dr. White to tell that Mark was in the hospital again they thought I was playing an April Fool's Day joke. Mark was kept overnight to make sure his heart was back in rhythm and his medications were adjusted to stabilize his heart. He had another heart catheterization to make sure there were no more blockages that could cause more damage.

We found ourselves constantly coming before the throne of Christ and trusting on His promises. When we looked at the storm around us, we felt so defeated. We persistently had to recall that we belonged to Christ.

> *"But now thus says the Lord, he who created you, O Jacob, he who formed you, O Israel: Fear not, for I have redeemed you; I have called you by name, you are mine. When you pass through the waters, I will be with you; and through the rivers, they shall not overwhelm you; when you walk through fire you shall not be burned, and the flame shall not consume you. For I am the Lord your God, the Holy One of Israel, your Savior. I give Egypt as your ransom, Cush and Seba in exchange for you. Because you are precious in my eyes, and honored, and I love you, I give men in return for you, peoples in exchange for your life. Fear not, for I am with you; I will bring your offspring from the east, and from the west I will gather you." - Isaiah 43:1-5*

Whenever we looked to the Lord, we would find peace in our hearts. We knew that God was in control. We began to breathe a little easier.

On July 4, 2004 we learned that Mark had a blood clot in his lung. I knew that a blood clot meant death could happen very quickly. Every time I tried to pray I would struggle trying to accept the pending doom. I called Dr. White that evening to help me make decisions. I knew that he would not lie to me when things were bad. Dr. White told me to trust God and trust him with this one. He thought that if Mark made it through that night he would be okay. His advice was to maintain my composure and to stay close to God. He told me all we can do is pray and let God do his work and we will take one day at a time. I could tell that Dr. White was worried but he kept me at ease. The week that Mark was in the hospital Dr. White kept in close contact with us, encouraging us to trust God and Mark's doctors with his care.

Mark required another heart catheterization, which showed weakness of the heart muscle. Another spell in January 2005 caused the cardiac surgeons to place the defibrillator quickly. At that time, also the American Medical Association stated in reports that they were finding defibs placed in heart patients with heart failure were faring better with the device in place. Just having the defib in place gave us a peace of mind. If his heart were to go out of rhythm or stop beating the defib could assure us he would get "a stiff kick in

Would could be better that the Easter Bunny!

the chest" that should hopefully re-start his heartbeat or bring it back into rhythm.

I called Dr. White on April Fool's Day 2005 two days after Mark had his defibrillator put in, and said that Mark was having trouble with his heart. He was upset that Mark was having another spell and said he was coming over. After listening to him get all shook up I told him that I had fooled him. After calming down he told me he would never believe me on April Fool's anymore!

What happened just a few months later, however, wasn't anything we could laugh about. In the summer of 2005 Mark and I decided that our family should go on a retreat with the Joni and Friends ministry which serves people and families with disabilities. The retreat was in Pennsylvania and the theme was around celebrating Christmas:

"I have come into the world as light, so that whoever believes in me may not remain in darkness." - John 12:46

Christmas had always been a very challenging time for me. I told Dr. White I wasn't sure that I could go; I was afraid. He kept telling me to go and be open-minded to whatever happened. He felt it was time for me to start healing instead of fearing Christmas. I promised him I would.

The week started out well. The ministry paired up the boys with buddies to go around with them during the week. Joel's buddy was Steven; Steven went to every event with Joel and worked with him on learning to eat. I remember being surprised to see Joel reach up for Steven to carry him. Joel usually is not cordial to people at first; he is in his own little world in his autism and he rarely lets people into his circle. Richard was also given a buddy named Kevin but we were concerned because Richard would take advantage of him, wanting Kevin to do everything for him.

The week was pleasurable. I learned that I could be happy at Christmas and see Christmas in a different light. I found myself having an exceptionally delightful time. I really grasped the genuine meaning of Christmas through the speaker, Pastor Kirby. I felt like Christ was telling me that it was time to move on and not be disheartened anymore. It meant that I could start living again. Cyndy would not want me to always be sad at the holidays. I needed to remember that she is not sick, that she is with the Lord, that she is enjoying herself, and that she is able to do things she never could do here. Praise God!

However my praise would quickly turn to pleading with God for my husband's life. All week something was making me feel uneasy about Mark. I thought his heart problems were making me nervous. One evening Katie and I were away from the building where the family was staying when Mark, Richard, and Joel went back to get ready for bed. Something made Katie go back to check on Dad and to let him know where we were. She raced back to get me. I couldn't believe what was waiting for me when I got back to the room. Mark was lying on the floor of the room covered with blood. Richard had assaulted him. My heart leapt into my throat. Was my husband dead?! I could not believe that the blood thinners that Mark was on to save his heart, were now threatening his life by preventing his wounds from clotting. I could not see myself living without him. Suddenly I turned against God. I had trusted Him and now He was about to take my husband away from me?!

Mark was airlifted to a trauma center 90 minutes away from the retreat site. When I was able to calm down I felt a voice telling me that He has not left me and to trust Him to get me through this ugly nightmare. A peace beyond understanding came over me. I began to see how God's knowledge and timing around the accident. There were three emergency medical people that were near the building when Mark was hurt; they were able to stabilize him get him airlifted to the right hospital.

Different people from the Joni and Friends ministry came to the hospital to help me through the long night and into the next day.

Even when I was angry I never felt like I was out of God's hand. He got my attention and held me tight. I was far from my own territory and away from family and friends; I had to lean totally on Him and not on myself. There was a peace when I put my hand into Christ's hand and trusted Him to carry me through each and every day of the two weeks that Mark was in the hospital. God provided all my needs during that time. I can say that I liked being in His hand.

About a week after returning home Mark's dad was admitted to the hospital. He was diagnosed with colon cancer. The night before his surgery to remove the tumor my brother-in-law talked with Dad and asked him, "if something happened during surgery or afterwards would you be ready to meet God?" Dad told Billy that he was but he was praying that God would give him more time with his family. He told Billy that if he was to die he knew he would be at home with the Lord.

Dad survived the surgery but was in grave condition. Our family was under a lot of stress. I prayed daily for Dad to get well. It seem like he was getting better but then ended up in the ICU for a week on the ventilator. I watched Dad fight for his life. He reminded me a lot of Cyndy.

Mark and I were going to visit Dad on a Monday morning. Coming down the hall I heard the death rattle and a disturbing feeling came over me. All I could do was pray that it wasn't Dad. I was moved to prayer when we got past the nurse's station and saw one of Dad's doctors. He caught Mark and I and told us that Dad was having problems.

Rushing down to Dad's room we got there before he slipped into unconsciousness. Dad grabbed my hand did not let go. He had gone into septic shock and aspirated. All I could do was plead with Dad to keep breathing and pray to God to let Dad live. We could see that Dad and Cyndy were kin – she had gotten her fight to live from him! Dad fought hard for the next six weeks of his life and returned from near death.

A week before the end of October we visited Dad at the transitional hospital. He was there to be weaned off the ventilator. While we were there his call bell started buzzing and would not stop. We kidded Dad that it was Casper the friendly ghost visiting him. With a serious look on his face Dad told us that Cyndy was doing that. We didn't think about it again until a week later.

Two days before Dad died we noticed he was looking up at bright lights in his room and talking to them and pointing to something up in the air. We didn't question Dad but later realized he might have seen Cyndy, his parents, and most of all His Savior. About a minute before his heart stopped Dad opened his eyes and looked up and smiled. He was not afraid to die. He knew he was going to be with his Savior. His life here on earth was over. He knew that he would be healed of the cancer. Dad was off the vent at last.

Fifteen minutes after Dad entered eternity I went back into the room to tell Dad goodbye. I cradled his head in my arms and laid my head on his; I was crying when the nurse told me to lay his head down and look at his face. He was smiling. It was the same smile I had seen numerous times over the last couple weeks of his life. I knew that Dad had done what I asked of him 90 minutes before he died - I had asked him to give Christ a hug for me along with Cyndy.

The smile on Dad's face helped me to get through the days leading up to his funeral. My heart was broken that Dad was gone but I knew he had asked the Lord to give me grace to get through his funeral. The peace I had, I knew without a shadow of doubt was from the Lord. He was holding me tight. I could feel the arms of Christ around me. Without His help I would not have made it through the funeral. I knew also that the family was holding me up in prayer because they were worried that I would not do well. Mark's brother Bill preached at the funeral.

These end of life experiences I have seen with our loved ones who knew the Lord has been a testimony to me; they have shown me that our God is real. He has a very tender heart. I also noticed how our Lord gives us every chance to get right with Him before we go. I would have loved to have been there to hear when Christ told Cyndy, Dad, and my Granny and Granddaddy "Well done my good and faithful servant," and "...come unto me." Wow!

> Dear Dad,
> You showed me what a loving father is. Thank you for letting me see Christ in you. Your last actions here on earth showed me that you were a child of the Lord's. Now rest peacefully my sweet Dad and take care of our Cyndy. We shall see you both in Heaven shortly.
> Love,
> Anne

When life seems to be at our worst we need to have faith in God to get us through one more day, week, month and year. With God we can do anything.

> *"And Jesus answered them, 'Have faith in God. Truly, I say to you, whoever says to this mountain, 'Be taken up and thrown into the sea,' and does not doubt in his heart, but believes that what he says will come to pass, it will be done for him. Therefore I tell you, whatever you ask in prayer, believe that you have received it, and it will be yours. And whenever you stand praying, forgive, if you have anything against anyone, so that your Father also who is in heaven may forgive you your trespasses." - Mark 11:22-26*

Death is no longer a problem when we know Christ as our Savior.

> *"And I heard a loud voice from the throne saying, 'Behold, the dwelling place of God is with man. He will dwell with them, and they will be his people, and God himself will be with them as their God. He will wipe away every tear from their eyes, and death shall be no more, neither shall there be mourning nor crying nor pain anymore, for the former things have passed away.'" - Rev. 21:3-4*

I really envy Cyndy, Dad, and my grandparents who have testified to me for they are seeing these things already.

Prayer

Thank you Lord for watching over us in our darkest hours. Thank you for loving us even when we are not lovable. Thank you for your Son who died for us that we might live life to the fullest, and then enter into your presence after death.

In Christ's name,

Amen

CHAPTER SEVENTEEN

Rejoice in Hope of the Glory of God

"Through him we have also obtained access by faith into this grace in which we stand, and we rejoice in hope of the glory of God. More than that, we rejoice in our sufferings, knowing that suffering produces endurance, and endurance produces character, and character produces hope, and hope does not put us to shame, because God's love has been poured into our hearts through the Holy Spirit who has been given to us." - Romans 5:2-5

One night a few years ago I heard news about a friend who had lost one of her children in an accident. Just the mention of her child's death brought back feelings of anger, shock, and pain. Over the past 14 years I have had numerous flashbacks of when Cyndy died. The feelings of anger and disbelief and shock come and go as I relive those moments. Pain can become unbearable until you come to terms with death. When your child dies you still have to go on with your life, one day at a time.

When Cyndy died, I felt like my heart was being ripped into shreds. People would come up and tell me they knew how I felt but they could not know exactly how I felt because it was not their child. That was my daughter that had died. Even if they had lost a child each person is different. You can help a grieving parent just by being there and listening; you can't tell them that you know how they feel. Well-meaning people often encourage their grieving friends to get over it – to live for the future and not dwell in the past. I had friends say "you don't need to worry about Cyndy anymore; she is gone." The friends were well-meaning but their words hurt me ever so deeply. Yes, my daughter is gone, but not forgotten. She will never be forgotten. She is just a memory away. Fifty years from now the memory of that very day will feel like it was yesterday.

I have found over the years that God alone truly understands what I am feeling. He, too, was a Father who had a child die--His precious Son Jesus. For a while, I was angry with God and had a real hard time dealing with my loss. I did not want anything to do with God. I could not understand how a loving Father would hurt me by taking my daughter away from me. Yet He was the one who could comfort me and help me through the roughest days and nights.

Only God can give true comfort and peace. In the Bible, God gives us His "911" chapter for times of extreme sorrow--Psalm 91:1-16. God tells us that He is our refuge and our fortress. When we hurt, He covers us with His wings. He will be our shield. He also has His angels surround us and watch over us when we are in pain. That particular scripture has been enormously comforting to me; it has helped me move forward with life and put my trust in God.

God gave me my space, but He let me know that He was there for me if I needed Him. He would always be there for me, no matter how hard I tried to push Him away. The only way to be able to get from day to day is to lay your grief on the Lord's shoulders and let Him bear your pain. He will give you rest and allow you to heal.

When I think about not being able to bear anymore, Isaiah 40:8 comes to mind: "The grass withers, the flower fades, but the word of our God will stand forever." God's word—his truth and promises—remain eternal, even when our circumstances cause us to doubt and fear. When I have become weary and need a lift, my heavenly Father gives me a hand as He said in Isaiah 41:9-10:

> "You whom I took from the ends of the earth, and called from its farthest corners, saying to you, 'You are my servant, I have chosen you and not cast you off'; fear not, for I am with you; be not dismayed, for I am your God; I will strengthen you, I will help you I will uphold you with my righteous right hand."

Isaiah talks about how God lifts us up when we are weary and heavy-laden. In Isaiah 43:1-2, he states that I am God's own and He sees the pain I am going through with the loss of Cyndy. He continues to watch over me in the midst of my pain.

> *"But now thus says the Lord, he who created you, O Jacob, he who formed you, O Israel: 'Fear not, for I have redeemed you; I have called you by name, you are mine. When you pass through the waters, I will be with you; and through the rivers, they shall not overwhelm you; when you walk through fire you shall not be burned, and the flame shall not consume you.'"*

Isaiah 40:28-31 is another incredibly encouraging passage for me:

> *"Have you not known? Have you not heard? The Lord is the everlasting God, the Creator of the ends of the earth. He does not faint or grow weary; his understanding is unsearchable. He gives power to the faint, and to him who has no might he increases strength. Even youths shall faint and be weary, and young men shall fall exhausted; But they who wait for the Lord shall renew their strength; they shall mount up with wings like eagles; they shall run and not be weary; they shall walk and not faint."*

God promises us that He will be there for us in our sorrow. Sometimes when my heart is heavy I think about how different my life would be if I had known or could have done something differently the day of Cyndy's death. The truth is I COULD NOT have changed what happened. There was no way I could have stopped Cyndy from dying. I had to realize that even if Dr. White were standing over Cyndy in that moment, he could not have done anything to stop her death. God alone has control of life and death.

It has been 14 long years since I lost Cyndy. The holidays are a very trying time for me. I often go back through all the stages of grief. There have been times when I feel like no time has passed since I lost Cyndy and that I am just beginning to grieve her. When those horrifying memories of her lying on the floor with the purplish bluish color in her face, or seeing her in the casket, or watching the casket being closed for good come to mind, I turn to Jesus and ask Him to take my hand and replace those memories with ones of good times we had with Cyndy. When my grief is so deep that I want to leave this old world behind and join Cyndy, Jesus gives

me the reason for living. The grief we suffer here on earth is short and will pass away; the joy we will have when we enter eternity has no end.

Christmas season 2004 when I was visiting with Dr. White I broke down in tears over the upcoming holidays. He has never seen me so upset. Later he admitted that he was scared when he saw how desperate I was feeling. Before he would let me leave his office Dr. White made me promise that I would not do anything to end or damage my quality of life. When I talked with him closer to New Year's Day, he reminded me that Cyndy is in heaven and that she is completely happy now. He reminded me that I will see her again and we will never be apart once we are safely home with the Lord. My only choice was to let go and to give the grief and pain over to Christ yet again. Now I am able to move on and trust God. Yet, there are times that I am like the little girl that takes the baby doll to daddy to fix the broken doll yet, when daddy takes the doll to fix it; I want my baby doll back even when daddy has not quite finish fixing it.

I know that I will see my daughter again, and when I do, what a day that will be! I will see my Lord and He will show me my healed daughter, made whole in glory. What a blessing!

I have found that it will take years to recover - if you ever recover - from a child's death. There will be times that you slip back in depression. It seems like every couple years I will have difficulty in dealing with Cyndy death. I have had to have my antidepressants changed. I have been told by several doctors that I would never come off antidepressants. However if we keep our faith in Christ, even when the storm is brewing around us, we will see that Christ alone will pick us up and safely place us on the other side. So when those category five hurricanes are coming over us, we may feel like there is nowhere to go and the water is coming up touching our feet, look up to the heavens because Christ is there. He will take our hand and led us through our roughest times in life. He is there we just have to ask him for help!

We still celebrate Cyndy's birthday every year. We buy a gift (flowers or balloon), and take it to her grave, and have cake and ice cream, as we would have done if she were still alive. On special holidays, we put flowers on her grave. At Christmas, we would put special ornaments that Cyndy made on our tree, or ones made in memory of her by her sister and brothers. We still hang her stocking on the fireplace and place a wreath on her grace with something new and creative added each year. We write her letters letting her know that we miss her and wish she were with us. These things really make it easier for us to remember her; none of us forget her.

We know that we will see our Cyndy again when we meet Jesus our Lord. We know that we have lots to catch up on when we see her! Time will have stood still for Cyndy even though many years here on earth will have passed since she went to God. We will enjoy God's creation and no longer be separated from each other or have any tears. God is so good to us!

Now I will try to live my life looking forward to the second coming of Christ or my death, whichever comes first. When I close my eyes here on earth for the last time, I will open them fully in the most peaceful, joyful place. No more sickness or sorrow will be in heaven. There will be no parting over there.

Pastor Harrell emailed me once that "there are too many Christians who want to make a straight and fun-filled line to the joy and glory of the Lord, when in fact, the Lord tells us in His word that it is THROUGH many tribulations that we enter the kingdom of Heaven. Our God does not intend to lead us around the furnaces of affliction, as though we would be consumed in them. Rather, He leads us through them, knowing that He will be with us in them and bring us out of them better than we were before we went through them."

Fourteen years later and counting, we can see the hand of God in our lives and hold our heads up high because we know that our Lord and Savior will get us through the worst circumstances that can happen to our families. The death of Cyndy was the worst and most stressful thing that ever could happen to us, yet Christ knew we would follow Him even though we suffer and complain along the way. When we are sent through the furnace we will come out on the other side without being harmed because we are drawn closer to Him who has molded and polished us to be a testimony of God. Cyndy is safely home with her loving heavenly Father and awaits us coming to join her even if it is 50 or 70 years. We will see her and the reunion will never end! As the hymn goes, even after ten thousand years we have no less years to see Cyndy and sing the Lord's praises.

If you know Jesus then you can have real hope in the midst of despair. There is comfort in knowing that God is in control, and that He does not give us more than we can bear. He watches over us and meets our needs and He cries with us when we cry over the death. If you have lost a child God wants you to remember that your child is with Him, and he or she is not suffering or sick anymore. He has made your child whole in Heaven. Your child is living in God's presence, praising Him for all His mercy and His loving kindness. God does not force Himself on us. He does not try to make things better superficially. He gives us room to grieve, but He is always ready to step in and give you His shoulder to lean on and His hand to hold. He is our perfectly loving Father.

Again, I will say that WITH CHRIST, I HAVE EVERYTHING and WITHOUT CHRIST, I AM NOTHING. I do not understand everything that Christ does but I know it is for a good reason. God healed Cyndy when He called her home on January 1, 1997. Cyndy became more alive and is able to do things she could not do here. She is more alive now, sitting with Christ at the right hand of God the Father. Cyndy dines at the table with Him. She sings praises to our Father: "Blessed assurance! Jesus is mine! Oh, what a foretaste of glory divine! Heir of salvation, purchase of God, born of His Sprit washed of His blood. Perfect submission--all is at rest. I in my Savior am happy and blest: watching and waiting, looking above, filled with His goodness, lost in His love."

Wow! When I think about what Cyndy is doing now, it does my heart good, but still there is that sadness that she is no longer here on earth. Yet I give the Lord thanks that she is in better hands and that she is no longer in pain. She is free from sickness and is able to walk and talk. The greatest blessing of all is that she belongs completely to the Lord. She is known as one of His children. Nobody can pluck her out of the hands of the Lord now. She is safely at home forever more.

Prayer:

Lord Jesus, thank you for loving us so much, and giving us comfort when there seems to be no comfort or peace of mind over the loss of our child. Lord, you know what you are doing. I sometimes have no clue of what you are doing. I try to second-guess you and figure out how losing my precious child has any place within Your perfectly good will. Show me your plan in the way that I will understand better, and help me to trust You even when I don't understand Your ways.

In Christ,

Amen

CHAPTER EIGHTEEN

For God Has Prepared For Them
A City Called Heaven

"But now they desire a better country, that is, a heavenly one: wherefore God is not ashamed to be called their God: for He hath prepared for them a city." - Hebrews 11:16

Since Cyndy's passing I can't say that I'm free. I will always carry a dull ache in my heart. Our family misses Cyndy a great deal. When we take the other children to Dr. White for checkups I still feel like we should be bringing Cyndy for hers, too.

But I am a witness of God's abundant grace for our family. Without a doubt, we have been drawn into a vibrant, closer relationship with our Heavenly Father. Our hearts are more in tune to His voice, and we see His hand in our lives. He is constantly working in our hearts for the betterment of tomorrow and our family. Our life is not easy but with God's strength, we can get through one day at a time.

We have learned time after time to draw our strength from Him as in Psalm 19:14,

"Let the words of my mouth and the meditation of my heart be acceptable in Your sight, O Lord, my Rock and my Redeemer."

Sometimes Dr. White calls me his rock; now I know where he gets it. He would tell me whenever I get upset that I was his rock—strong and unwavering in faith. My husband Mark would tell him the rock has some chips, but remains strong. Thank you, Dr. White, for encouraging me to stay strong even when the storm is raging around us. There are times when he wants to get some cement and seal the cracks so the rock won't crumble to dust. Yet, Dr. White no matter what I do he just does his best to show me the love of the Lord and that he cares about me. Sometimes when I get into my unstable moods I am not sure why Dr. White sticks so close to me. I am shown Christ's love time after time through Dr. White. He has a strong influence on me when it comes to my Savior and family. I know that I can always turn to him and he will tell me how to proceed with a godly attitude in life.

There are still days when it is very hard to give praise to the Lord. There are still days I just cannot pray. That is when the Holy Spirit offers up prayers for me. I have to rely on Psalm 46 to help me see that God is with me, as my help, in the time of trouble.

"God is our refuge and strength, a very present help in trouble. Therefore, we will not fear though the earth gives way, though the mountains be moved into the heart of the sea, though its waters roar

and foam, though the mountains tremble at its swelling. There is a river whose streams make glad the city of God, the holy habitation of the Most High. God is in the midst of her; she shall not be moved; God will help her when morning dawns. The nations rage, the kingdoms totter; he utters his voice, the earth melts. The Lord of hosts is with us; the God of Jacob is our fortress. Come, behold the works of the Lord, how He has brought desolations on the earth. He makes wars cease to the end of the earth; He breaks the bow and shatters the spear; He burns the chariots with fire. 'Be still, and know that I am God. I will be exalted among the nations; I will be exalted in the earth!' The Lord of hosts is with us; the God of Jacob is our fortress."

I hope I have made clear in this entire book that God is my strength; only He will enable me to go on with my life. Without Christ, I am nothing. I cannot function from day to day without having a relationship with Jesus. There are still times that I just want to end my life because of the intensity of my grief and pain. There have been times I know that I would have taken my life but Christ had to be holding me back from trying anything or foiling my attempts. There was one time when I knew I had taken enough medications that if it did not kill me that I would at least be severely physically damaged. Yet it was not my time to meet my Lord. I know without a doubt that God is the reason I am still here today. Those times are when my faith is at its lowest. Yet, Christ holds me close to His heart. I believe this with all my heart—NO ONE can make it through the death of a child WITHOUT God.

Having a relationship with Jesus does not mean that we don't go through trials. Remember that Christ suffered, and He was without sin. Peter had wise words about our sufferings:

"Beloved, do not be surprised at the fiery trial when it comes upon you to test you, as though something strange were happening to you. But rejoice in so far as you share Christ's sufferings, that you may also rejoice and be glad when his glory is revealed. If you are insulted for the name of Christ, you are blessed, because the Spirit of glory and of God rests upon you...when we suffer as a Christian, let him not be ashamed; but let him glorify God on this behalf." - 1 Peter 4:12-14, 16

During the difficult days, weeks, months, and years after Cyndy's death, I had to keep my focus on Christ. I tried to memorize Scripture or remind myself of God's promises in His Word. Knowing that I could not bear this load alone, I forced myself to reveal my heart to Jesus. I needed Him to carry my burden, as the Bible says in 1 Peter 5: 6-7--

> *"Humble yourselves, therefore, under the mighty hand of God so that at the proper time He may exalt you, casting all your anxieties on Him, because He cares for you."*

Because I know my time on earth is temporary, I look forward to the reward waiting for me in heaven. I will see my Savior face to face and will see my Cyndy again. I love how Peter talks about our faith and the grace we have in Christ:

> *"Resist him, firm in your faith, knowing that the same kinds of suffering are being experienced by your brotherhood throughout the world. And after you have suffered a little while, the God of all grace, who has called you to His eternal glory in Christ, will Himself restore, confirm, strengthen, and establish you." - 1 Peter 5: 9-10*

What an awesome promise we have in Christ!

As I reflect on Cyndy's attitude about her life, she never complained about being unable to speak or how she could not walk well. She had a mind of a two-year-old and acted as if she had no worries. She was content with the way God made her. Even when Cyndy was sick and had to be put into the hospital she showed the love of Christ to her doctors and nurses. She was always happy to see her doctors, especially Dr. White and Dr. Garrison. She would show her love by clapping, cooing, and blowing kisses to them.

If you do not know Christ I strongly urge you to earnestly and honestly seek Him. He gives us our only hope of ever seeing our children again. And walking with Him is the only way we will be able to live our lives to the fullest with our children gone before us. Jesus is our ONLY source of peace we will have here on earth. Again, I say WITHOUT CHRIST we have NOTHING. It is only WITH CHRIST we have EVERYTHING. Without suffering and pain, we will have no compassion on humanity. WITHOUT CHRIST, we grieve as if there will be no tomorrow.

Just recently, I took Dr. White to see someone that served with him as Cyndy's pallbearer. The friend we were going to see was dying of cancer. On the way back up to the church, Dr. White looked toward me with a puzzled look on his face and said that he just could not see how people make it through life without Christ. A Christian has hope because they know if that their love one had Christ in their hearts, they will see their loved one again. A person without Christ has no reason to hope.

When our life here on earth is over, we have a home to go where there will be no sickness or pain or sorrow. We will see our Savior face to face and never have to part from our loved ones anymore. I love the last two chapters in Revelation that paint a glorious picture of heaven. Most importantly, we will be with our Savior, face to face:

"They will see His face, and His name will be on their foreheads. And night will be no more. They will need no light of lamp or sun, for the Lord God will be their light, and they will reign forever and ever." - Rev. 22:4-5

This reminds me of the song "Shall We Gather by The River." In Revelation, John also speaks of the crystal water and gold streets we will see:

"Then the angel showed me the river of the water of life, bright as crystal, flowing from the throne of God and of the Lamb through the middle of the street of the city; also, on either side of the river, the tree of life with its twelve kinds of fruit, yielding its fruit each month. The leaves of the tree were for the healing of the nations." - Rev. 22:1-2

Thinking of heaven makes me want to hurry there. Our time here on earth is very short when we think about being with Christ for eternity. Cyndy has been gone for years, but when we see her in glory, all that time that she wasn't here on earth with us won't even matter anymore. We will be together forever. And even the joy of being with Cyndy would not compare to the amazing joy of being with our Savior Jesus Christ for all time. May we long for heaven, our true home, and trust in our God to bring us safely there.

Prayer:
Thank you Lord for our salvation and loving us when we are not lovable. Thank you for giving us everlasting life. When this life is over, thank you for promising us a home, where there will be no sorrow or pain. We will be with our loved ones forever. We will be with You forever.
In Christ,
Amen.

CHAPTER NINETEEN

Cyndy's Blessed Assurance

*"He will wipe away every tear from their eyes, and death shall be
no more, neither shall there be mourning nor crying nor pain anymore,
for the former things have passed away." - Rev. 21:4*

Over the last 14 years Mark and I have faced countless trials.
Our beautiful daughter died suddenly. Mark had a massive
heart attack and could no longer work. Our second oldest autistic son nearly killed Mark, Sr. during a trip away from home. My
father-in-law battled with, and finally succumbed to, cancer. Just within
the past year my youngest sister Cathy was diagnosed with a brain tumor. It is to her that this chapter is dedicated.

The night Cathy called to tell me the news about her tumor we had a
severe thunderstorm. We had just prayed as a family when my daughter
Katie went to call some of her trusted friends asking for prayer. She came
back screaming for us to come outside and look. As I went out I saw a
beautiful rainbow stretch across the sky with a bright spot in the middle.
The next morning when I saw a picture of the rainbow on the computer I
saw where the bright spot was Christ's fingers holding the rainbow in the
clear sky. I felt surpassing peace. I knew that our prayers had been heard.
God was telling us to trust Him - that Cathy is going to be just fine. I've

had to place this in the hands of Christ because I could not fix this problem. It is too giant of a problem for me to fix.

Sitting on her Christmas loot.

Watching God's plan play out has been such a blessing. Christians from all over the world have been praying and God has poured out His blessings on my sister's family. When people say 'there is no God,' I really pity them. They have no idea what they are saying. God has provided all Cathy's family's needs. People have come out of the woodwork to help her and her family. Now if that isn't God then who is God? May God get the glory for what He has done for my family. May we continue to lean on Christ and may our faith in the Lord becomes even stronger than we have ever known. The doctors were able to remove all but .5% of Cathy's tumor; she returned from the hospital within two days of the surgery and has no lasting effects from the tumor.

As I have pondered the Lord's faithfulness, I have seen how Dr. White has stood beside us through it all over the past 20 years. He would follow each new Harrell baby and help guide us regarding what would be the best care for each of them. He was the one to tell us that our precious daughter Cyndy was going to be leaving for Heaven soon. He was there with us when our last child Joel was born prematurely and needed neonatal care. In life and death Dr. White has remained close to us.

On May 18, 2005, I got a surprising phone call from a local NBC-TV station about an article I had written about the profound effect Dr. White had on our family. It had been six months since I had written it and really didn't think anything would come of it. To our surprise the TV station wanted to give Dr. White a shining star award for all that he has done. Now Dr. White is not one to draw attention to himself. He is fearful of being in front of crowds yet Mark and I were able to encourage him to do it. My family really felt very blessed that he would do the show for us. When I was looking over the pictures that were taken at the filming I noticed his smile. It really told of the happiness and joy he experienced that day. Finally my family had a way of letting him know just how appreciative we were, and are, of his support over the years. Those pictures were worth a thousand words.

Two years later on May 18, 2007, I was working on my family ge-

Dr. Larry White, reluctant shining star.

nealogy when I discovered that Dr. White and I are distantly related! We knew we were close but neither of us really knew why we cared so much about each other. To be honest, he has felt like close family member – even an older brother to me – over the whole 19 years of knowing him.

When I think about being related to Dr. White, I think about what Cyndy knows being in Heaven. I know she and Dad looked down and smiled at my shock over discovering that Dr. White and I are distant cousins. I understood then why I often felt moved to pray for him. Our God is so good and true to us.

Now I can truly understand why the Lord had chosen Dr. White to help write the dramatic book about Cyndy's life and death and healing process. He told me that he was honored that I would ask him - of all her doctors - to help. He encouraged me to write about things in my life that I didn't think had any significance or bearing to the book only to realize later that they did. I don't know how many times I would just beg him not to make me write about something that hurt, and he would say that writing it would help my health both mentally and physically.

There are times when I genuinely caused him heartache and he should have turned his back on me but he didn't. He would just shake his head, reflect on the unconditional care of Christ, and forgive me. He lives Proverbs 16:32:

> *"Whoever is slow to anger is better than the mighty,
> and he who rules his spirit than he who takes a city."*

He is always tender even when I have hurt him. Over the 10 years that we have been writing this book I have seen how the Lord has changed and blessed me. I have learned to trust Christ with all my heart and soul. I can see where the Lord was just preparing me to be able to handle the ministry He has in store for me. I have been challenged to

148

pray for people including my dear friend and co-author Dr. White. I have had to learn to trust people, to be more loving, and to live life as to if today was my last day here on this earth. I have also looked toward tomorrow to see my daughter once again. When I do see her again I will not have to worry about parting from her ever again. When I have breathed my last here the pain of losing my daughter is gone forever.

Prayer:
There is so much Lord that we have to be thankful for. Thank you for the friendships you have given us with different ones. Thank you for the blessing they are in our lives, the lessons they teach us Thank you for your eternal love that one day we will be joined back together with our love ones that have gone before us. Thank you for the joy of having coauthors, and the friendships that grow from them. May you take this book now and give the reader the joy you have given us over the years and the assurance of your unconditional love and care.
In Jesus Name,
Amen

EPILOGUE

It has been 14 years since Cyndy went to be with the Lord. Our family has grown and changed. Our friends continue to support us, and we are blessed to support them. Today we all continue to experience God and His blessing in many different ways:

Mark has lived longer then the doctors thought he would. His heart doctor cannot believe that it has been 12 years since Mark's heart attack and that his heart is still stable. Mark and I are in our 27th year of marriage and still very much in love.

Mark Jr. is 26 years old and living in a Christian group home for adults. He works at CSS in Chesapeake (a sheltered workshop) preparing the cables for cable TV. He is very happy and has made a lot of progress over the years. He calls us daily and we enjoy talking with him.

Richard is 23 years old and lives in an adult group home in our neighborhood. He works and enjoys his job. He loves going to church with Katie on Sundays and plays basketball in the Special Olympics.

Buddy is 19 and lives in a group home for children with behavioral problems. He is doing much better. He has told us since he was six years old that he wants to be a trash collector. Well maybe that will happen! At least now we can let him out the door and not worry about being yelled at for him wanting to help the garbage men!

Joel is 16 years old and is also disabled in some of the same ways as Cyndy, but not as severely. He is in an autistic program in school. He will now make eye contact but is very meek. He has begun to look a lot like Cyndy.

Katie graduated from high school on June 11, 2008. She enjoyed JROTC while in high school and received several awards. I know that her angel – Cyndy – was very proud of her for finishing school. As I watched my youngest daughter marching in to the auditorium with all of her classmates, I could not help crying. My job of raising Katie was finally finished. When she was born, Mark and I dedicated her to the Lord and asked that she be used to further His kingdom. Now it's time to see how well Mark and I have done and raising her to be a servant of the Lord's. Katie has gone on several mission trips with the church and wants to go into missions when she finishes college.

Dr. Garrison is still practicing medicine and is still following our youngest son Joel.

Dr. White is entering his 35th year as a physician and 25th as a child neurologist. He is excited about the advances in treatment of muscle diseases, epilepsy, and genetic disease, yet concerned about the availability of care to some people, the ever-growing costs of health care and an apparent unwillingness of some to adjust styles of living which will remain a formidable challenge. He hopes to still be around to see stem cells change the world.

As for me I have been in college for the last two years working toward a Bachelor of Arts with a double major in English and Journalism and Communications. I will graduate in the spring of 2013. I am also thinking about a second book to write.

Again I give God the GLORY for ALL HE HAS DONE IN OUR LIVES. Without God I will not be where I am today. The Lord has provided every single need for my family. And I thank God for all He does - and will continue to do - in our lives. Dr. White and I pray that this book has touched your life as much as we have seen the Lord touch us.

God Bless You!

THE OMEGA

After the echoes of his mother's last words faded into silence, the little angel gazed at her in wonder and surprise. "How do you feel, my darling?" he heard her say.

He began to think. God blesses us. God blesses us all. Love God or ignore God or even curse God and He loves and blesses us the same. Unconditionally, we are all blessed by God, whether we know it or accept it. Like with Cyndy's Mom; she knows it. Dr. White knows it.

We began to think some more, and as he did he noticed the outline of his mother, brilliant white against a blue sky, next to him on his right. As he turned the other way he saw an outline of a young girl, slightly older than him, shimmering a bright yellow; and he thought she was smiling. The girl in the story!

Now thoughts were rushing in like a tidal wave. Jesus was sent by God to tell us and to show us the way – to let us know that the way is through him. He is our assurance that God is always there for us, no matter what. Now he understood! Blessings are from God. Strength and guidance are from Jesus. And He is part of both!

As those realizations sank in, he began to notice his surroundings change. As the outlines of his mother and the girl with the curl sharpened, he began to recognize they were not alone. He saw his large angel, Eugene, a few steps to his right, nodding and smiling. And there were others.

He looked up at his mother. "You were taken from life too soon, my love," she cooed. "But now you know and have accepted the truth; now you are with us."

As he looked out beyond her he began to recognize shapes, then faces. More and more of them, silhouetted against a blue sky that reached forever. There must have been millions...or more. Then the angel Eugene raised both arms upward and boomed "Let all rejoice! Heaven has a new member!"

As a group of voices as diverse as the universe rejoiced "hallelujah" and then began a chorus of "This is My Story," the little angel heard a voice from his left. "My name is Cyndy," the little girl with the curl whispered, "with a Y. Isn't this cool?"

All he could do was nod. He was with God! God was with him! As he looked out on millions and millions of faces that were glowing brighter by the second, he realized he knew them. He knew them all! And he felt warm and full and loved all at once!

Over the din of the singing he could still hear his mother's soft voice asking "Are you all right, son? How do you feel?" Looking to his right and then to his left, he replied: "I feel wonderful, mama. I'm where I belong. I'm home."

CPSIA information can be obtained at www.ICGtesting.com

262567BV00001B/5/P

9 780976 593270